The Pacific Century

Staffan Burenstam Linder

THE PACIFIC CENTURY

Economic and Political Consequences
of Asian-Pacific Dynamism

STANFORD UNIVERSITY PRESS
Stanford, California

Stanford University Press
Stanford, California
© 1986 by the Board of Trustees of the
Leland Stanford Junior University
Printed in the United States of America
Original Printing 1986
Last figure below indicates year of this printing:
96 95 94 93 92 91 90 89 88

CIP data appear at the end of the book

353709

0 8 04713057 c
C

For Thesy and Peder—
companions on Pacific tours

Preface

Pacific vitality and vigor offer the world as a whole the opportunity to create a good future, and the task of understanding and representing the political and economic implications of this dynamism, for the Asian-Pacific countries themselves and the other countries of the world, is an important and a challenging one. It takes a lifetime to become an expert on any one of the many and highly diverse countries of the Pacific Basin, and though I do not claim to have that expertise, I do think it possible to understand enough of what is happening in this rapidly changing region to illuminate the likely consequences for the rest of the world, whether for the established industrial countries in Europe and North America, for the developing countries, or for the communist camp.

My background in economics and in elective political office has stimulated and guided my interest and work in this field. During two periods and a total of eight months in 1983-84, I had the privilege of being invited to use the excellent research facilities of the Hoover Institution, Stanford University, California, where a substantial part of my work on this essay was carried out. I profited greatly from discussions with and encouragement from many Stanford economists and political scientists, among whom I wish to mention Nathan Rosenberg and Daniel I. Okimoto. My wife Thesy and my young son Peder tell me that they had an excellent time at Stanford, and this too helped me greatly. Extensive travels in the Asian-

Pacific region—beginning with a lecture tour in Japan in 1963 and including an all-too-short period at the National University of Australia in Canberra in 1982—and the advice and help of many people throughout the region have been a necessary and pleasant part of my work.

I gratefully acknowledge the generous support I received from the Marianne and Marcus Wallenberg Foundation during the writing of this essay.

S.B.L.

Contents

Tables

But you cannot help but feel that the great Pacific Basin, with all its nations and all its potential for growth and development—that is the future.

President Reagan in an interview in
Far Eastern Economic Review, May 17, 1984

The Pacific era is a historical inevitability.

Prime Minister Nakasone in a radio
speech, Nov. 20, 1984

If the capitalist system is not guaranteed in Hong Kong and Taiwan, prosperity and stability there cannot be maintained.

Vice Chairman Deng Xiaoping, Beijing,
Oct. 15, 1984, as quoted by Xinhua News Agency

ONE

A Pacific Century?

This essay explores the implications of a force that is transforming world politics and economics, namely the dynamism manifested in the Pacific region. Since the early 1960's the Pacific Basin has been undergoing more rapid economic advances than ever before. Its spectacular growth in production and international trade and its overall economic attainments have brought about a shift in the world's political and economic center of gravity.

The world is becoming more complex, with an increasing number of actors on the global stage. The new actors—Japan, the Asian newly industrializing countries (NICs), the Association of the Southeast Asian Nations (ASEAN), and most recently China, as well as the whole Pacific region as such—have been claiming and getting a larger role for themselves. As a result, the political and economic influence of the various world powers, groups, and blocs is being redistributed.

The successful Pacific countries are all market economies with private entrepreneurship and private property. They give considerable attention to efficient allocation by way of rational prices, and they have an outward-oriented development strategy focused on international trade. The success of the Pacific countries means that other regions are experiencing a relative decline as their share in world activity falls. This decline will prove especially difficult for countries that rely on a different economic system from that of the successful Pacific countries, since in addition their strength will be sapped as the attractiveness of the system declines both at home and abroad. Already there are signs that their own self-confidence is eroding, and they are experimenting with reform. This is exactly what is happening in China, and because of China's political prestige the reforms there will reverberate throughout the other socialist and communist countries. And many leaders in developing countries will find it easier to discern the progress of the capitalist Asian-Pacific countries and to draw new conclusions. Pacific growth has a powerful ideological effect.

The relative decline of other market economies, however, manifested in a growth rate lower than the Pacific Basin's, is compensated for by a strengthening of the position of market economies in general. The Pacific examples are persuasive. Time-honored methods are becoming fashionable and are imitated. In the struggle between systems and ideologies the established industrial countries are faring well. Furthermore, these countries can derive benefits from Pacific growth. For open economies, there will be a wider scope for mutually beneficial trade and factor movements as the world economy enlarges. There will be bigger markets and better sources of supplies. Opportunities for international investments will increase, flows and transfers of technology will expand, and new economic policies and industrial methods will be employed. The new stimulus from competitive forces will cause not only a useful reallocation of resources but also an intensified search for improvements and innovation. Pacific growth invigorates.

The market economies in North America and Western Europe, in particular, are well placed to derive benefits from these opportunities. Nevertheless—and here is the problem for the established market economies—the gains from trade will not be automatic. For the gains to be fully realized, the old economies must respond vigorously. They must thrust themselves into new activities, including a reallocation of factors of production. In practice, however, such adjustments seem to be painful, particularly in Western Europe. Countries fettered by severe constraints on factor mobility, which thus have a low capacity to take initiatives and to make adjustments, see new threats rather than new opportunities in the phenomenon of Pacific growth and competition. These negative perceptions may carry over into destructive economic policies, damaging both the established countries and their trading partners in the Pacific.

This is also a political problem for the established industrial countries. Instead of deriving benefits from an enlarged partnership with an emerging economic power, they may convert the relationship into one of friction and antagonism. Furthermore, a great many countries beyond the Pacific region, attracted by powerful examples, are hesitantly experimenting with reforms and more outward-oriented trade strategies. By responding negatively, the established countries may risk frightening away these developing nations, making it more difficult to achieve a reorientation and to discard inward-looking policies aggressive toward the industrial West.

The task for the established industrial countries should nevertheless be much simpler than for the socialist and communist countries. To meet the Pacific challenge, the established market economies have only to accept a structural readjustment of resources, whereas the socialist and communist systems must readjust both their political beliefs and their economic structures.

The Pacific countries have demonstrated that growth is not a miracle. Underdeveloped countries in East Asia have followed Japan and have become, in a real sense, developing countries. Indeed, the Asian-Pacific NICs have shown that it is possible not only to achieve vigorous growth but to challenge the established industrial countries and even, like Japan, to reach out for leadership. This Pacific phenomenon is revitalizing the world. In global terms, center and periphery do not exist in some eternal arrangement. At the beginning of the post-war period there was much optimism about possibilities for economic development, followed by much disappointment as the strategies in vogue proved unhelpful or even disastrous. But now, in the Pacific, alternative policies have been tried—the very policies, in fact, that once gave the rich countries their affluence. It is exciting to see these policies succeeding again. It gives grounds for much new hope—if only the alternative, but proven, ways are not obstructed by the established, threatened countries, pursuing policies harmful to all.

A Pacific Profile

In economic terms, the most important of the northeast Asian (or northwest Pacific) countries is Japan. Indeed, it is the most important actor in the Pacific region as a whole, an economic superpower (see Tables 1 and 2 below). Three smaller northeast Asian countries—South Korea (hereafter referred to as Korea), Taiwan, and Hong Kong—form, with Japan, an Asian-Pacific hub. Along with Singapore, these three countries make up the group of successful newly industrializing countries of Asia (NICs), whose spectacular growth shows greater resilience than that of the South European and Latin American NICs.

The important southeast Asian (or southwest Pacific) countries are Thailand, Malaysia, Singapore, Indonesia, the Philippines, and newly independent and oil-rich Brunei. These countries, joined together in ASEAN, form an important part of the Pacific economy. Singapore is not alone in having put in a strong performance. The other four big ASEAN countries belong to a group of "new exporting countries" (NECs) that have achieved an even faster growth rate in manufactured exports during the 1970's than the celebrated NICs.

Also a part of the Pacific Basin are the South Pacific countries of Australia and New Zealand–like Japan, members of the Organization for Economic Cooperation and Development (OECD)–and Papua New Guinea.

The sheer size and weight of China and its ancient civilization mean that its presence is very much felt in the region, and the Chinese diaspora gives this presence an added dimension.[1] A communist economic system, however, and an inward-looking strategy have reduced China's regional presence and influence. In spite of a considerable internationalization of the economy since Mao's death, China still has less foreign trade than Taiwan; China's total exports and imports in 1983 amounted to U.S. $43 billion, U.S. $2 billion less than Taiwan's. The direction China chooses will nevertheless be of the greatest significance for the future position of the Pacific in the world economy.

The other communist countries in the area are represented only geographically and militarily. The USSR has its civilian and its economic face turned to Europe–in fact, even more so than most of the wholly European nations. Siberia, with its long Pacific coastline, is an enormous Pacific back yard. It is administered as a territory, however, by the Russian Republic, one of the State Republics, which has its headquarters in Moscow under a purely European leadership. Vladivostok, Irkutsk, and other Soviet cities in Siberia are European cities, built by Europeans for inhabitants who are predominantly Europeans. As Malcolm Mackintosh explains in a paper on Soviet attitudes toward East Asia, "Whatever role the Soviet Union seeks to play in Asia, and whatever aims and interests it may have there, they belong to a European and global power in Asia and not to an Asian power acting on Asian political and social assumptions and using Asian negotiating techniques."[2]

Like the Soviet Union, North Korea and Vietnam have a strong military presence in Asia, but they are economically introspective. Economic failure has kept them small. They are military exclamation points and economic parentheses. Their economic importance lies solely in the contrast they provide. These countries (along with Laos and Kampuchea, which are occupied by Vietnam) will therefore be excluded from our discussion of the Pacific or Asian-Pacific region.

In contrast, the western regions of the United States and Canada play a substantial role in the Pacific economy. California and the other western states are surely no Pacific back yard. The "westernization" of the United States in economic vitality and population density is a significant factor in the growing importance of the Pacific Basin. In 1950 total personal income of the five Pacific states of the United States was 28 percent of that of the eighteen Atlantic states. By 1960 it had risen to 35 percent, and by 1982 to 42 percent. Similarly, the population of the Pacific states increased from 30 to 37 percent of that of the Atlantic states between 1960 and 1982.

Because the North-American West, that is, the East Pacific, is well integrated with the West and South Pacific, it is possible to speak of a Pacific Basin economy and to make comparisons and contrasts with the Atlantic economy. The United States faces both the Atlantic and the Pacific, and it will be significant which way it looks with greater attention. If Asian-Pacific growth causes the United States to focus rather more on the Pacific, this focus will serve to reaffirm the global economic realignment, even though U.S. interests make the country not so much an integrated part of a dynamic Pacific Basin economy as a separate entity in a very special relationship with the Asian-Pacific community.

The Latin American countries bordering the Pacific are not at present intensively engaged in the Pacific economy, although here too one can discern a growing awareness of Asian-Pacific opportunities. This shift is noticeable in Mexico in spite of all the local economic activity set off by the oil discoveries in the Gulf of Mexico.

The island states of the South Pacific,[3] the trust territories under the United States and France, and the islands associated with New Zealand are all very small, and their number and their economic insignificance make it statistically convenient to omit them from this presentation. Their relevance in other contexts should not be neglected, however, deriving as it does from "the importance of being unimportant": their small size makes them politically exposed. Since taking them over would be relatively inexpensive, they are potentially interesting to powers ambitious to establish a regional presence but constrained by inefficient economic systems and overtaxed economic resources. Australian foreign policies and aid policies are in part designed to contain such risks.

Table 1 provides an economic profile of the countries of the Pacific Basin. Japan is not the most populous country in the region, and certainly not the biggest, but it has almost half of the region's GDP. China, in spite of its massive size and population, accounts for only one-ninth. (As noted in the table, however, Chinese GDP may be underreported in international statistics.) The U.S. Pacific states account for 18 percent of the region's total GDP. All the other members of the region, with the exception of Australia, account for less than 5 percent each.

To study the interaction within the Pacific, it is instructive to divide the region into subgroups, as shown in Table 2, which gives figures for the subgroups in relation to world totals. For comparison, data are also given for the United States as a whole, for Europe (OECD), and for the non-Pacific less developed countries (LDCs). It should be noted that there are certain overlaps among the Pacific subgroups. Japan is listed separately but is also included in Northeast Asia; Singapore belongs to both the Asian NICs and ASEAN; and Papua New Guinea is included both in the South Pacific group and also among the LDC's of the Asian-Pacific region.

In the subsequent discussion of the interaction of the Pa-

A Pacific Century?

TABLE I
Population, Area, and Income of Pacific Basin Countries

Region	Population (millions, mid-1982)	Area (thousands sq. km.)	GDP (billions U.S.$, 1982)	GNP per capita (U.S.$, 1982)	Share of total Pacific Basin GDP, 1982
Japan	118	372	1,062	10,080	46.8%
Korea	39	98	68	1,910	3.0
Taiwan	18	36	46	2,500	2.2
Hong Kong	5	1	24	5,340	1.1
Singapore	2.5	1	15	5,910	0.7
Malaysia	15	330	26	1,860	1.1
Thailand	49	514	37	790	1.6
Indonesia	153	1,919	90	580	4.0
Brunei	0.2	6	4	20,000	0.2
Philippines	51	300	40	820	1.8
Papua New Guinea	3	462	2.4	820	0.11
Australia	15	7,687	164	11,140	7.3
New Zealand	3	269	24	7,920	1.1
China	1,008	9,561	260	310	11.5
U.S. Pacific states	32	2,386	406	12,280	17.9

SOURCES: World Bank 1984. Data for Taiwan from Republic of China 1984. Data for Brunei from U.N. ESCAP 1984 and Far Eastern Economic Review 1984. Data for the U.S. Pacific states (California, Oregon, Washington, Alaska, and Hawaii) from U.S. Bureau of the Census 1984.

NOTE: World GDP (U.S. $9,749 billion) does not include Eastern Europe. The data given by the World Bank for the GDP of China are unusually uncertain. Since 1977 the Bank has given a much lower figure for the Chinese GDP than, for instance, the U.S. Bureau of the Census in its international section of *Statistical Abstract of the United States*. For unreported reasons, Beijing has asked the World Bank to revise downwards its estimates of the GDP of China. Possible explanations of this phenomenon may be that China wants to position itself for reporting bigger strides ahead after the introduction of new economic policies, or for keeping down its dues in various international organizations, or for soliciting concessionary credits. The U.S. *Statistical Abstracts* put the Chinese GDP for 1980–the last year it lists–at $552 billion. This figure is the same as the CIA (1984) provides for that year in its *Handbook of Economic Statistics*. This Handbook also revises the Chinese GDP downwards for 1981 and 1982. For 1982 the CIA reports China's GDP to be $300 billion, a figure that is still substantially higher than the World Bank figure. For 1983 the CIA has a figure of $342 billion.

cific Basin region with other regions of the world, reference will be made to the Asian-Pacific group, which is made up of the first thirteen countries listed in Table 1. It consists of the Pacific Basin region with the exclusion of the U.S. Pacific states (because of the special global interests of the United

States) and of China (because of the different economic system obtaining there).

As Table 2 shows, the Pacific Basin accounts for almost one quarter of world production, but (because it includes China) a much larger proportion of world population. If instead we look at the Asian-Pacific countries, we can see that their share of world production (16.5 percent) is much higher than their share of world population. Comparing these figures with those for the United States and Europe, we find that although the Asian-Pacific region is still far behind economically, it has made considerable progress.

TABLE 2

Share of Various Asian-Pacific Groups and Groupings and of the United States, Europe (OECD), and Non–Asian-Pacific Basin Late-Developing Countries (LDCs) in World Population, Area, and Income

Region	Population		Area		GDP	
	Millions, mid-1982	Percent of world total	Thousands sq. km.	Percent of world total	Billions, 1982	Percent of world total
Japan	118	2.6%	372	0.3%	1,062	11.0%
Northeast Asia	180	3.9	507	0.4	1,200	12.4
ASEAN	271	5.9	3,070	2.4	212	2.2
South Pacific	21	0.5	8,418	6.5	190	2.0
Asian NICs	65	1.4	136	0.1	153	1.6
Asian-Pacific LDCs (excl. China)	336	7.4	3,667	2.8	352	3.6
Asian-Pacific region	472	10.4	11,623	8.9	1,602	16.5
China	1,008	22.2	9,561	7.3	260	2.7
U.S. Pacific states	32	0.7	2,386	1.8	406	4.2
Total Pacific Basin	1,512	33.2	23,570	18.1	2,268	23.4
United States	232	5.1	9,363	7.2	3,010	31.0
Europe (OECD)	407	8.9	4,273	3.3	2,968	30.6
Non–Asian-Pacific LDCs	2,117	46.5	63,254	48.4	1,722	17.7

SOURCES: Same as for Table 1.

The Economic Shift: Total Income

A comparison of the recent economic performance of the Pacific region with that of other regions shows that the center of gravity of the world economy is indeed shifting from the Atlantic Basin to the Pacific Basin. As can be seen in Table 3, the GDP of the Pacific Basin rose between 1960 and 1982 from 16 percent of world GDP to almost 25 percent. In the same period, there was a spectacular rise in the ratio of Pacific Basin production to Atlantic Basin production from about 40 percent to about 60 percent. If we look at just the Asian-Pacific region, we can see that its share of world production has doubled between 1960 and 1982. The ratio of Asian-Pacific GDP to U.S. GDP has risen from 18 percent to more than 50 percent. The increase in relation to European GDP is not as large, but is still remarkable. This increase in the rela-

TABLE 3
Changes in Various GDP Ratios, 1960-1982

Ratio	1960	1970	1980	1982
Asian-Pacific GDP over world GDP	7.8%	11.5%	15.5%	16.4%
Pacific Basin GDP over world GDP	16.2	20.0	21.6	23.3
Pacific Basin GDP over Atlantic Basin GDP	38.5	45.9	49.4	57.3
Asian-Pacific GDP over U.S. GDP	18.0	29.7	58.4	53.2
Asian-Pacific GDP over European GDP	27.5	37.4	43.9	54.0

SOURCES: Same as for Table 1, except that the GDP figures for 1970 are from OECD 1984b and U.N. 1983.

NOTE: World GDP does not include the GDP of Eastern Europe. Pacific Basin GDP is Asian-Pacific GDP plus the GDP of China and total personal income of the five Pacific states of the United States. Atlantic Basin GDP is European (OECD) GDP plus total personal income of the eighteen U.S. Atlantic states. As pointed out in the note to Table 1, the World Bank estimates of the GDP of China probably represent an undervaluation. If we use the figures given by the U.S. *Statistical Abstract*, the Pacific Basin GDP over World GDP for 1980 would be 24.6 percent instead of 21.7 percent; the Pacific Basin GDP over Atlantic Basin GDP for 1980 would be 56.4 percent instead of 49.4 percent.

tive economic significance of the Asian-Pacific region is also evidenced by the region's having contributed to upwards of 20 percent of the total increase in world production during these years.

As we have noted, Japan's GDP makes up a dominating part of Asian-Pacific GDP. In 1960 it was 47 percent of the area's total GDP; in 1970 it had risen to 69 percent. Since then, however, this ratio has remained stable or even declined somewhat. In 1982 the ratio stood at 66 percent. Thus the increasing significance of the Asian-Pacific region and of the Pacific Basin as a whole cannot simply be attributed to the rapid growth of Japan.

Projections

How far-reaching the effects of the Pacific Basin's rapid growth will be will depend on whether that growth continues. As can be seen in Table 4, the worldwide shocks of the 1970's and the deep recession in the early 1980's actually caused a decline in the growth rates of the Asian-Pacific countries. Nevertheless, growth there was still much faster than in other regions. In 1982-84 the growth rates of many Asian-Pacific countries outstripped those of Europe by a greater margin than ever, and they exceeded even that of the United States, in spite of the phenomenal economic upturn there. (Because of the rapid increase in the exchange rate of the dollar, however, Asian-Pacific GDP has not risen in dollar terms compared with the U.S. GDP. The ratio of Asian-Pacific GDP to that of Europe (OECD) is estimated to have risen to 60 percent by the end of 1984.)

In any evaluation of the growth potential of the Asian-Pacific countries, many problems for the future must be recognized. In spite of the strong economic performances of these countries, their socioeconomic and political situations are not idyllic, and should not be idealized. Thailand, Korea,

TABLE 4

Past and Projected World Growth Rates and Projected Economic Gravity Shift

Region	Average annual GDP growth rate							Percent of world GDP, 2000
	1960-70	1970-80	1982	1983	1984	1985	2000	
Japan	12.4	4.6	3.3	3.0	5.8	5.0	4.4	13.5%
Asian-Pacific NICs							6.0	2.6
Korea	8.9	9.5	5.3	9.3	8.4	6.5		
Taiwan	9.3	9.8	3.4	7.1	9.6	5.7		
Hong Kong	13.7	9.3	1.1	5.9	9.0	5.8		
Singapore	9.4	8.5	6.3	7.9	9.4	6.4		
Other A.P. developing countries							4.0	2.4
Philippines	5.2	6.5	3.0	1.4	-1.9	1.3		
Indonesia	3.4	7.6	2.2	3.1	3.6	3.3		
Malaysia	5.9	7.9	5.2	5.8	6.3	5.3		
Thailand	8.3	7.2	4.1	5.8	6.1	5.9		
Established industrial countries							2.5	1.7
Australia	5.4	2.9	0.7	0.6	6.3	2.3		
New Zealand	3.9	2.0	1.0	3.8	2.5	-0.5		
Total Asian-Pacific								20.2
China	4.5	3.2	-2.1	3.7	6.8	3.0	4.0	3.1
United States	5.5	4.0	-4.4	3.3	4.3	2.8	2.5	27.6
Canada	4.8	2.9	0.7	1.3	2.3	2.5	2.5	2.6
Europe (OECD)	4.8	2.9					2.5	27.2
Non-A.-P. LDCs	5.5	6.0					4.0	19.3

SOURCES: Growth rates for 1960-81 from UNCTAD 1983b. Growth rates for Taiwan from Republic of China 1984. Growth rates for Brunei and Papua New Guinea are not available. Growth rates (actual, estimated, and projected) for 1982-85 for industrial countries from OECD 1984a. Growth rates for LDCs for 1982 from Asian Development Bank 1984, for 1983-85 from Nomura Research Institute, *Quarterly Economic Review* (Aug. 1984): Table 6.1, p. 43. Past growth rates (but not the projected share of World GDP) of "other LDCs" include growth of the developing Asian-Pacific countries. The projected growth rates to the year 2000 are taken from *Japan in the Year 2000* (1985: 38-41). They are calculated with 1982 as the base year. World income in the final column excludes the GDP of Eastern Europe.

NOTE: If we use the higher U.S. Bureau of the Census (1984) estimates of Chinese GDP for 1980 as a base in our projections, the Chinese share of World GDP in the year 2000 would be 6.4 percent instead of 3.1 percent. This would give the Pacific Basin as a whole a higher percentage of world GDP.

and Taiwan have serious foreign policy problems. There are shadows over the future–and thus the present–of Hong Kong. Considerable domestic economic and political problems exist in the Philippines. In some countries there is a potential for racial conflict. Moreover, the growth of protectionism in industrial countries is the foremost economic problem for the whole region, further inhibiting strategy of growth through trade.

For Japan, there are many less serious, but significant, limitations. Technology can no longer be imported and improved, but must be created. The population is rapidly greying, a change that will increase the ratio of dependents to productive workers and may also cut into the savings ratio. Higher standards of living may erode the work ethic. Government expenditure is rapidly increasing in relation to total expenditure, with the result that the efficiency of the economy may suffer. The industrial policy of discriminating against small firms may restrict the capacity to experiment so essential for moving beyond mere duplication. Similarly, a weak venture capital market may hamper Japan's search for her future.

Nevertheless, most observers agree that Pacific growth will probably continue to surpass that of other regions. This view is expressed both in qualitative evaluations and in formal econometric studies. If the view is correct, the resultant shift in the world's economic center of gravity will have a transforming impact on future decades. Even small differences in growth rates can cause dramatic changes in the relative economic influence of the major industrial regions of the world.

The past and projected growth rates in Table 4 illustrate a predicted continuation of the shift in distribution of the world's income. The projections are from *Japan in the Year 2000*, an ambitious semi-official report prepared under the chairmanship of Saburo Okita and published in 1983. It is described as the result of "182 meetings of 128 experts during a one year period." According to the scenario, presented in

Table 4, there will be a narrowing of the interregional gap in growth rates that has characterized the period from 1960 to 1985. Even as the gap narrows, however, there will be a further important economic shift toward the Pacific. According to the scenario, Asian-Pacific GDP will have risen from 15 percent to 20 percent of world GDP between 1980 and 2000. It will be 75 percent of the combined U.S. and European GDP—90 percent if one adds to it the Chinese GDP. And assuming a more realistic evaluation of China's GDP than that presently provided by the World Bank, it will actually equal the GDP of the United States and Europe by the year 2000. In other words, for the total production of the Asian-Pacific region (excluding China) to exceed that of the United States and Europe by the year 2000, the growth-rate differential would have to be only one-and-a-half percentage points higher than the one projected in this scenario; this differential would still be much smaller than that recorded between 1960 and 1984.

The Economic Shift: Trade Flows

Along with the redistribution of world income, there has been a parallel shift in trade flows. Our assessment of this shift will focus on the changing position of the Asian-Pacific countries. Since there are no separate trade statistics for the U.S. Pacific states, the United States must be treated as a whole. And China, which has pursued an inward-looking strategy, has a minor role in world trade.

As can be seen in Table 5, the ratio of Asian-Pacific exports to world exports doubled between 1960 and 1982. In manufactured exports the surge was even more marked. In the same period total Asian-Pacific trade (exports plus imports) surpassed U.S. trade by a wide margin, rising from 70 percent of U.S. trade to 130 percent. Asian-Pacific trade rose substantially in relation to European trade, even during the 1960's, when the formation of the European Economic Community

TABLE 5

Relative Changes in Asian-Pacific Trade Flow Ratios, 1960-1983

Ratio	1960	1970	1980	1982	1983
Asian-Pacific exports over world exports	9.0%	12.9%	15.3%	17.6%	18.9%
Asian-Pacific manufactured exports over world manufactured exports	8.7	14.2	19.9	20.4	
Asian-Pacific trade (exports plus imports) over U.S. trade	69.7	87.8	121.9	129.8	130.8
Asian-Pacific trade over European (OECD) trade	23.1	26.8	34.4	40.8	42.6
Asian-Pacific trade over trade of LDCs	43.2	68.8	50.5	55.5	59.4
U.S. trade with Asia-Pacific over U.S. trade with Europe (OECD)	48.1	70.8	97.8	109.5	122.3
EEC trade with Asia-Pacific over EEC trade with United States	61.9	50.2	70.3	68.2	71.7
Trade of Asian-Pacific LDCs over trade of the other LDCs (incl. oil countries)	21.7	30.0	28.8	34.3	39.9
Manufactured exports of Asian-Pacific LDCs over total manufactured exports of all LDCs	30.9	41.6	64.3	67.1	
Manufactured exports of Asian-Pacific NICs over total manufactured exports of all LDCs	24.2	36.2	56.2	58.8	

SOURCES: IMF 1963, 1975, 1984b. Data for trade in manufactured exports, from U.N. 1966, 1976, 1984, and GATT 1984. Taiwan data for 1980-83 from Republic of China 1984.

NOTE: The ten present countries of the EEC are included in the EEC statistics for 1960 although they were not all members at that time. "Manufactured exports" include SITC 5, 6, 7, and 8. U.N. 1984 does not give data on the manufactured exports of Korea, Malaysia, and the Philippines for 1982. Korean manufactured exports are assumed to have changed at the same rate in 1981-82 as those of Taiwan; the exports of Malaysia and the Philippines are assumed to have changed in parallel with the average for the other Asian-Pacific countries.

(EEC) and the European Foreign Trade Association (EFTA) precipitated a rapid increase in intra-European trade. As to the LDCs, oil price increases (and decreases) have had such a marked effect on the value of total LDC trade that relative changes here are less clear. But in the 23-year period surveyed here, there was a 50 percent increase in the ratio of Asian-Pacific trade to total LDC trade.

One remarkable and potentially significant development in the same period was the overtaking of U.S. trade with Europe by U.S. trade with the Asian-Pacific countries (see Table 5). There was also an increase, although a less spectacular one, in European trade with the Asian-Pacific region. Trade between the ten present members of the EEC and this region rose from 62 percent of EEC trade with the United States in 1960 to 72 percent in 1983. During the 1960's there was a considerable decline in this ratio, as a result of the reduction of U.K. trade with Australia and New Zealand when the United Kingdom joined the EEC. Since then, however, the ratio has risen substantially, and over the full period it is possible to detect a definite increase in EEC trade with the Asian-Pacific countries over EEC trade with the United States.

Another dramatic development is the change in the ratio of manufactured exports of the Asian-Pacific LDCs to total manufactured exports of all LDCs, which rose from 30 percent to more than 65 percent between 1960 and 1982. Still more striking is the increase in the ratio of manufactured exports of the four Asian NICs to total manufactured exports of all LDCs. The four Asian NICs, which have less than 2 percent of the total population of the LDCs, accounted for more than 55 percent of total manufactured exports of those countries in 1982 (up from 24 percent in 1960).

Three Effects on the Outsiders

The rapid growth in Asian-Pacific income and trade has not only transformed the region itself but has also had a substantial effect on other parts of the world. Our analysis will distinguish three principal effects. First, there is a message. Pacific success will provide a powerful demonstration effect; it will influence patterns of thought and economic strategies elsewhere. Amidst disillusionment, failed convictions, and capsized ideologies, it offers a model to be emulated, suggesting invigorating new approaches where none seemed available. On the political level, the success of the Pacific model may seem discouraging to countries and groups dominated by non-market ideologies. But whereas in some of these countries the old ideologies may simply be undermined, in others the demonstration effect may be such that they will be jettisoned in favor of a pragmatic reorientation. By the same token, the demonstration effect will be a boon to those countries and schools of thought that discover in the Pacific model a reinforcement of their own ideological convictions and a vindication of their own economic systems.

Second, Pacific dynamism will encourage broader and more substantive interregional partnerships. It will have a stimulating effect, especially on open, trade-oriented economies. Growing markets will provide new opportunities for the sort of international specialization that has increased the wealth of nations in the past. Pacific growth will provide other countries with new sources of capital and technology and new opportunities for direct investment. Macro-economic linkages will be formed by means of trade and factor movements. Furthermore, Pacific growth will provide the new competition necessary to prevent monopoly and stagnation and stimulate the search for improvement. If other countries meet the challenge with a dynamism of their own, Pacific growth will become a source of additional strength to their own economies.

Third, Pacific growth will have a threatening effect, since certain sectors of national economies are likely to suffer from new competition and the pressures and pains of adjustment even if the overall effects of that competition are beneficial. But it may also pose a more general threat. If the capacity to respond to competition is impaired by distorted economic policies and domestic trade obstacles, with a consequent decline in vitality, the effects will be far-reaching. Rents derived from technological leadership may be eroded. New opportunities may not be grasped. Workers unwilling or unable to adjust may find themselves unemployed. The new competition may provoke, not action and cooperation, but inertia and isolation—and if destructive, isolationist economic policies do prevail over those suggested by the demonstration effect, they may precipitate a global economic decline.

These three principal effects help us to explain and predict important developments and trends, and to discern the options and the opportunities to be weighed in planning for the future. An evaluation of these effects is important for the development of peaceful and profitable partnerships. The non-Pacific nations must develop constructive insights into how they can turn Pacific growth and change to their benefit, instead of submitting to negative reactions potentially damaging not only to themselves and the Pacific nations but to international relations in general. In projecting a growth trajectory for any country—and especially an Asian-Pacific country—the response of the international community to Pacific dynamism, together with the effects of that response on the international economy, is the most crucial (and the most uncertain) variable.[4]

Changes in the relative economic influence of countries and continents have occurred before, of course, and such changes have had their effects on past international configurations. To look back no further than the beginnings of the age of mass-production, we note how Germany overtook Great Britain, how the United States surpassed Europe, how postwar Europe caught up again, and how the Soviet Union progressed behind its own barriers. We note in particular how, at the beginning of the century, Japan emerged from feudalism and isolationism so quickly that alarmists cried out about the dangers of a "yellow peril" in the international marketplace. The dimensions of the present economic realignment, however, are quite different and still more dramatic.

"High Tech" and "High Ec"

Because of improved means of communication, the intensity of international interdependence is now greater than ever before. The propagation of impulses is faster, facilitating global interactions in which old and new industrial nations, advanced and developing countries, and economic superpowers are all engaged. In addition, a technological race that has important economic implications is heightening the ordinary competition for markets. Although techno-rivalry is not an unknown phenomenon, the possibility of a change in leadership in high technology—in sophisticated technologies that will permeate and dominate world production—is something altogether new.

Most importantly, there is not only a "high tech" race but also a race in "high ec." Different economic systems are on trial. There is competition not only in terms of production but also in terms of the system of production. With the rise of socialism, challenging the capitalist system that brought affluence to the first generation of industrial countries, the subject of economic performance became an ideological battleground. Leaders of socialist countries in particular anticipated economic victories that would lead to a conquest of minds. They expressly pointed to the Asian masses, arguing that the future for their system in Asia would be won by communist economic progress outperforming that of the capitalist West. Such claims are no longer heard. As the long-term evidence from the Asian-Pacific region becomes overwhelming, the strengths and weaknesses of alternative systems grow visible even through the mists of prejudice. These developing perceptions will have great geopolitical and geoeconomic significance.

For the established capitalist countries that have more extensive economic links to the Asian-Pacific nations than to other groups of nations, the two dominating effects will be the promise of wider partnerships and the challenge of new competition. For the socialist East, the threat of the demonstration effect will be primary.

In the South, engaged more in economic planning than in economic growth, reactions will be mixed; the agony of reversing policies and politics will be balanced by the excitement of implementing new, successful policies. For China, a constituent of both the East and the South, agony and inspiration will be blended in unusually strong doses, and the resulting chemistry will be of the utmost political and economic importance for the world in general. The Marxist manifesto notwithstanding, the end of socialism is perhaps more likely to be a reformed economy than an exalted communism.

The economic dynamics of the modern world can be characterized, then, as a dual competition in high ec and high tech. High tech is the culmination of the competition for markets; high ec is the culmination of the competition for minds. Japan is the brilliant rival of the capitalist West in high tech. The Asian NICs are the shining rivals of the communist East and socialist South in high ec.

TWO

The Demonstration Effect

The Japanese have borrowed extensively, but with skill and pride. The slogan adopted after the Meiji Restoration in 1868 was "Western technology and Japanese ethos": foreign technology would be adapted to indigenous values, and thereby strengthen the social fabric of Japan. Because the subsequent advances were so remarkable, defeat in World War II came as an especially severe blow to Japanese conceptions. The enormous economic successes of the postwar period, however, have permitted the Japanese to regain their self-confidence. Their recovery of poise has been pronounced—in the view of some observers, too pronounced. At any rate, the spirited tone of Japanese documents assessing the economic future differs sharply from the tone of gloom and doom prevalent in most other countries.

The semi-official study *Japan in the Year 2000* illuminates the country's current aspirations when it suggests that "Japan has the power to contribute significantly to the stability and vitality of the world from now on in a leading role among industrially advanced nations." After describing the need for an internationalization of Japan, the study goes on to say that "the first basic strategy for various problems emerging in the internationalization process is to render positive service toward revitalizing the world economy." Later it discusses "the practical use of Japanese economic vitality," and it devotes a section to the question of maintaining and promoting vitality in a maturing economy: "To positively maintain and shape such vitality [capacity to promote growth and ability to adapt to change] will be a fundamental condition for Japan to resolve various problems in heading for the 21st century. . . . It is important for all people who make up society to live energetically with spiritual satisfaction, and build a society full of vitality, even though this may not directly relate to productive activities." [1]

The same self-confidence characterizes the "visions for the eighties" formulated by Japan's Ministry of International Trade and Industry (MITI): "For Japan, the period of 'modernization for catching up with advanced Western economies' has ended, and the country is now about to enter the next phase of development." And again: "The day will come when Japan's vitality will be useful in preventing the whole world from falling into a prolonged slump." [2]

The Asian-Pacific region is tending less and less to look outside for impulses and concepts, turning its attention instead to models closer to home. By virtue of her success in challenging the "old hands" in the West in trade and technology, Japan has inevitably attracted most of the attention and admiration, even though bad memories linger and frictions continue. But Japan is not the only model. Some of the Southeast-Asian political leaders who have introduced an explicitly "look East" approach have not only Japan in mind but also Korea and (although not openly) Taiwan.

Rapid development in Southeast Asia and among the Asian NICs has engendered within the region a greater appreciation of its own capacities than is characteristic of, say, Africa or even South America. In recent years the Asian-Pacific countries have experienced an increasing specialization in goods and services as a result of foreign trade while tending toward greater self-sufficiency in ideas for progress. (Most developing countries have done the opposite.) These tendencies, which are not easily quantifiable, are nevertheless perceptible in reports and articles in East Asian journals and newspapers such as *Far Eastern Economic Review, Asia Week, Asia Wall Street Journal,* and the important Japanese financial press. For example, *Far Eastern Economic Review* of December 15, 1983, ran an article headed, "The emerging executive—signs are detected of the maturing of a specific Asian style of manager, though shortcomings remain." Reporting on a conference in Malaysia, the article mentioned that "Malaysia's Prime Minister, Datuk Seri Mahathir Mohamad, . . . offered some 'Asia-centric' views. He singled out the management element in his now familiar Malaysia Inc. and Look East concepts and welcomed management training as a boon to communities which had no tradition of commerce and industry—an apparent reference to Malaysia's bumiputra (indigenous race) majority. Mahathir added unequivocally that 'adoption of the Japan Inc. concept is the basis of our . . . Malaysia Inc. concept.'" The "Look East" policy has also been discussed in more academic treatises.[3]

Various Japanese writings reflect a similar confidence in the future of the whole region. The Japanese Pacific Basin Cooperation Study Group, set up by former Prime Minister Ohira, speaks of "the vast potential of this region not simply for the benefit of the Pacific countries but to enhance the well-being and prosperity of human society as a whole."[4] *Japan in the Year 2000* comments on the Pacific region as follows: "In the Pacific region surrounding Japan, there are many diverse countries possessed with the hidden possibility of developing greatly toward the 21st century by assisting each other. If economic solidarity progresses in this area and the region's potential power for growth is fully demonstrated, it is possible that the Pacific region will become the nucleus of revitalization of the world economy."[5]

These new apprehensions are not confined to economic issues. For instance, in drawing up social blueprints for the future, leaders in Korea and Singapore have sought to guard against what they identify as systemic weaknesses in the Western welfare states. The Japanese clearly share these concerns: "now that Japan has economically reached the level of developed nations and that socially the troubles of the West European-type welfare society are becoming clear, an economic society of the Western type can no longer be a model for Japan."[6]

There is no despair in the Asian-Pacific region. There is neither the geriatric gloominess of certain of the established industrial economies nor the learned helplessness of such developing nations as labor under the assumption that they are owed something by others. Economic success and the self-confidence ensuing from it form the basis of the demonstration effect. "If you do not believe in yourself, nobody will believe in you." Conversely, if you believe in yourself—and have reasons to believe in yourself—almost everybody will believe in you.

What Are the Lessons?

The importance of the economic system and economic policies of the Asian-Pacific countries in explaining their phenomenal growth has already been discussed. But many other, different kinds of explanations are also given. Some of them emphasize a "situational imperative" stemming from constraints peculiar to city states and to countries lacking natural resources. Others emphasize the driving force of the Confucian ethic, particularly as it affects immigrant minorities who are restricted to economic pursuits. And for Japan, the Japanese ethos—with its base in the Japanese variant of Confucianism—has been assigned a crucial role. Other explanations have stressed various institutional factors—in Japan, for example, an industrial policy and an industrial organization featuring *zaibatsu*, general trading companies, and bank-based industrial financing. Japanese success has also been attributed to a combination of such elements as a "search for consensus," the lifelong employment system, special managerial techniques, and built-in quality control.[7]

As economic progress in the Pacific region has become more widespread, however, it has become increasingly difficult to rely on particularized growth theories. The Pacific region is heterogenous. There are countries as wide from east to west as the United States, and there are city states. There are countries rich in natural resources and countries altogether lacking in such resources. There are both sparsely and densely populated countries. All the major religions are represented. Some countries are racially homogenous; others are multiracial, with or without accompanying friction. Some countries, such as Korea and Taiwan, are militarily exposed and devote much of their resources to defense; others, such as Japan and the Philippines, have low defense budgets; others, such as Australia, are simply remote and secure. Virtually all constitutional systems are represented, including the colonial government of Hong Kong and the republican government of "nonexistent" Taiwan. As heads of state there are emperors, queens, elected and hereditary kings, presidents, and generals. The various countries exhibit widely different levels of economic development and have highly different economic histories.

These differences are given special force by the enormous distances within the Pacific region. The Pacific Basin is much wider than the Atlantic Basin. The bankers of San Francisco are closer to the gnomes of Zurich than to the headquarters of the Hong Kong and Shanghai Bank. The distance between Tokyo and Singapore is about the same as between London and New York.

The great differences among the Asian-Pacific countries have made it increasingly difficult to account for widespread growth by means of sociopolitical and natural-resource-oriented explanations. The Japanese ethos is Japanese. As to

Confucianism, there are as many types of Confucianism as there are sects of the Christian creed. Furthermore, the practice of Confucianism is not always accompanied by modern economic growth. In China, where its values ought to be most deeply ingrained, there have been grave economic difficulties. Taiwan and Korea, which also possess strong Confucian values, did not experience rapid growth until the early 1960's. In fact, Confucian values have (at least since Weber) been viewed as inimical to economic growth. Though the achievements of Taiwan and Korea suggest that Confucianism and the old culture associated with it may, in the long run, facilitate economic growth once started, it does not trigger it. Like the Protestant work ethic in Western Europe, it can hardly be considered a necessary ingredient.[8]

Similar difficulties are inherent in attempts to attribute growth to the contributions of the Chinese. The Chinese communities in the Pacific countries have indeed been highly successful.[9] They have become so prosperous, in fact, that they have aroused some resentment. Discrimination against them is most evident in Islamic Malaysia and Indonesia, where interracial marriages are uncommon and dividing lines are consequently clearest. Nevertheless, some of the most successful countries have no Chinese population, and China itself, with its population of hundreds of millions, has yet to achieve rapid growth. If Chinese talents in themselves were of such importance, China—and not Japan—would be an economic superpower.

Similar difficulties beset attempts to explain Pacific growth by reference to particular Japanese institutions. It is highly likely that "the unique Japanese capacity to cooperate," the search for consensus, the Japanese in-house union system, and Japanese managerial methods have played a role in their own historical and psychological context. These same factors do not prevail in other fast-growing Pacific countries, however. Japanese growth ceases to seem so miraculous when compared with that of other countries in the region. Purely Japanese institutions accordingly become more interesting in an ad hoc growth theory than in a general one.

For the same reason, it is difficult to attach as much importance to Japanese industrial organization, industrial policy, and the activities of MITI as some political scientists do.[10] The proponents of the industrial policy argument do not have in mind an environmental type of industrial policy, one that attempts to function by means of economic stability, the establishment of stable game-rules, and support of education, training, and research. What they have in mind is an interventionist industrial policy, one in which supposedly wise and farsighted politicians and administrators phase activities in and out and decide which suns should rise and set, and when and in what fashion. This argument, however, cannot explain why some very successful Asian-Pacific countries such as Hong Kong and Taiwan have not needed to employ interventionist industrial policies on a large scale. And even in Japan it is doubtful that industrial policy interventions have been employed on a scale massive enough to explain Japanese growth.

As critics of the industrial policy argument observe, the mechanisms by which Japanese industrial policy of any magnitude have been carried out since the postwar regulations on trade and foreign exchange were lifted have never been adequately demonstrated. There is no planning linked to budgets. Sizable investment funds are channeled through public budgets, but an analysis of the allocation of these resources shows that most of them go to ordinary public works programs that are largely directed by local government. Similarly, the Fiscal Loans and Investment Program of the central government supports conventional causes such as housing, small businesses, national railways, and highways. The Japan Development Bank also has a conventional portfolio profile. Tax policies are only incidentally related to recognizable indus-

trial policy objectives. As in most countries, tariff policy pro-
tects (in a rather contradictory manner) some weak old-
timers as well as some hopeful newcomers.

Whatever the industrial policies that have been carried out,
it is also open to question whether Japanese industrial policy
interventions have been sufficiently far-sighted and future-
directed to validate the industrial policy argument. The U.S.
Council of Economic Advisers notes that the Japanese government and its councils of experts "have a mixed record of
success" and that the "net effect of [Japanese] policies on economic growth is not clear."[11] This is all the more true in-
asmuch as programs need not be failures to be expensive; the
industrial policy argument is often weakened by its failure to
consider the opportunity costs of various promotional programs. Since MITI officials are not omniscient, the costs in
terms of opportunities surrendered could be considerable—
even if there is less risk in Japan than in other countries that
industrial policy programs, supposed to assist the future, will
be hijacked by self-seeking forces preventing change.[12]

In short, the Japanese industrial policy argument cannot
explain all that is frequently asked of it. As Charles Schultze
persuasively puts it: "Those who attribute Japan's economic
success primarily to MITI's industrial policy seem to be suggesting that without MITI the huge 30 to 35 percent of GNP
that the Japanese have invested in the past several decades
would have gone mainly into such industries as textiles, shoes,
plastic souvenirs, and fisheries. This is sheer nonsense."[13] In
Korea, industrial policy interventions have been far-reaching
but have been subjected to similar criticisms and they can
hardly have provided the mechanisms for growth. Indeed,
heavy-handed industrial policy measures during the latter
part of the 1970's are often regarded as the cause of considerable economic difficulties during that period.[14]

These observations are not meant to suggest that industrial
policy has had no effect on Japanese industrial structure, but

only that this effect could not be the whole story. The supposed blessings of Japanese industrial policy have received too much attention and have been given too much importance, even by those who usually put no faith in the constructiveness of interventionist economic policies. This infatuation has proved particularly strong when misaligned exchange rates and depressed business conditions have created political pressures that can be eased by finding a scapegoat and by magnifying the effects of targeting and of the alleged unfair advantages enjoyed by foreigners. It is at such times that the attractions of a cure-all around the corner—with its promise of somehow avoiding painful readjustment, dedicated work, and the complex tasks necessary to achieve macroeconomic balance—become unusually great.

Economic Explanations of Asian-Pacific Growth

With so many instances of success to account for, increasing attention has been given to the economics of Asian-Pacific growth. Although economic policies and institutions differ within the region, there are certain basic commonalities. The Asian-Pacific countries are all market economies. Price structures are not heavily distorted and principally reflect opportunity and production costs. Resources are efficiently allocated (or at least the importance of efficient allocation is well understood). All the countries pursue an outward-oriented export strategy. Private property and entrepreneurship are part of the system, which affords considerable economic freedom. Savings and investment ratios are high. There is reasonable confidence that the quality of government is acceptable and that the capitalist rules of the game will not be erratically changed or be destroyed.

To be sure, there are also considerable differences in the economic policies of the Asian-Pacific countries. There is the laissez-faire economy of Hong Kong and the substantial industrial policy interventionism of Korea. In some countries outward-oriented trade policies take the form of free trade; in others, of "double distortions," consisting of export promotion subsidies aimed at offsetting cost disadvantages from ordinary protectionism. Efficiency is sometimes so much impaired by protectionism that there is negative value added. This is true of the Thai auto industry, where the value of the finished product is less than the combined costs of the inputs. Again, confidence in the stability of the rules of the game may waiver, as in the Philippines or—for very special reasons—in Hong Kong. In some countries, Indonesia for instance, the fabric of regulations is still so thick that it requires the payment of much "gate money" to speed up the decision process, and this in turn causes fierce competition among rent-seekers, who attempt by means of persuasive gifts to obtain the windfall profits that government licenses and permits will bring them.

Yet such differences, important as they are, are not sufficiently great to set this group of countries off from most of the less developed countries of the world. An index of LDC distortions in the pricing of foreign exchange, factors of production, and products (as calculated by the World Bank for the 1970's) places even Indonesia in a group of countries with fairly low distortions. Among the six countries with the lowest price distortions, we find Thailand, Korea, Malaysia, and the Philippines (along with high-growth Malawi and Cameroon). In contrast, the six countries with the most extensive distortions are the relatively unsuccessful Argentina, Chile, Tanzania, Bangladesh, Nigeria, and Ghana.[15] (It should be noted that Hong Kong, Taiwan, and Singapore are not included in the calculations; if they were, they would certainly lead the group with low distortions.)

A point made by Chalmers Johnson about interventions in Japan may have a bearing on developments in other Asian-Pacific countries too. Johnson distinguishes between "developmental" and "regulatory" interferences, and claims that

Japanese policy makers intervene in order to strengthen the market forces, not to combat them.[16] Interventionism, in the sense of regulatory interference, is limited in Asian-Pacific developing countries because they lack the mistrust of markets and private entrepreneurship that motivates large-scale doctoring in other Asian countries and in African and South American countries.

In assessing the importance of the economic policies pursued in the Asian-Pacific region, it should be remembered that Korea and Taiwan experimented for a number of years with a system of planning and import substitution under which they experienced slow growth and great difficulties. Not until extensive policy reversals were introduced toward the end of the 1950's and the early 1960's did the spectacular takeoff begin. Toward the end of the 1970's, the Korean government again stepped up its interventions, attempting to force through a number of extremely capital-intensive projects. These efforts backfired, precipitating an economic setback followed by another reduction in interventions. On the whole, Korea's interventionist policies have resulted in lower savings and a more expensive and capital-intensive growth than Taiwan and Hong Kong have experienced.[17] Korea has had to rely much more on the international capital markets to finance its growth. Nevertheless, the sum of Korea's "double distortions" is much less than the distortions of the inward-looking policies of most developing or undeveloped nations.

It is noteworthy that even Singapore had an initial, mild flirtation with inward-looking policies. But when Singapore was forced out of the union with Malaysia, the notion that its growth could be organized on a Malaysian home market was shattered. When the present, free-trade policies were instituted, a much higher rate of growth was realized.

The countries in the region that have held to diametrically opposed development strategies—the socialist countries—remain wretchedly backstage. In their failure to "arrive" economically, they offer a striking contrast with their neighbors. Of the market economies in the region, the only one that has not experienced rapid growth is New Zealand. The country has been plagued not only by agricultural protectionism abroad but also by substantial self-imposed protectionism. Its domestic markets have also been obstructed by government and union interventions.

It is impossible to elaborate here on the economic policies of all the Pacific countries. Some economic policy characteristics can be inferred, however, from the indicators compiled in Table 6. The countries with the highest income growth rates (as shown in Table 4 above) also have the lowest price distortions, the smallest government sectors, and the highest savings, investment, and export growth rates.[18]

Although there are differences in emphasis, these relationships are given prominence in the rapidly growing literature on the economic policies of Japan and the successful Asian NICs.[19] The benefits of an export orientation have been given special attention.[20] Bela Balassa sums up the research on the subject. "The evidence is quite conclusive," he says: "countries applying outward-oriented development strategies had a superior performance in terms of exports, economic growth, and employment, whereas countries with continued inward orientation encountered increasing economic difficulties. At the same time, policy reforms aimed at greater outward orientation brought considerable improvements in the economic performance of countries that had earlier applied inward-oriented policies."[21] One of the classical benefits of trade is better resource allocation. Thus the Asian-Pacific countries have avoided, for instance, the discrimination against labor-intensive agriculture that has typified many other planned economies bent on "industrialization." As various studies have shown, a more efficient allocation of resources and economies of scale has been accompanied by dynamic gains from trade. Trade encourages competition, which intensifies re-

TABLE 6

Economic Policy Indicators for Asian-Pacific Countries,
Selected Years, 1960-1982

Country	Percent of GNP				Annual average export growth rate	
	Total central government expenditure, 1981	Savings, 1982	Invest- ment, 1982	Exports, 1982	1960-70	1970-82[a]
Industrial market economies						
Japan	19%	31%	30%	15%	17.2%	8.5%
Australia	25	20	22	15	6.5	3.8
New Zealand	40	21	25	29	4.6	3.9
AVERAGE	28%	20%	20%	19%	8.5%	5.6%
Upper middle- income LDCs						
Korea	19%	24%	26%	39%	34.7%	20.2%
Taiwan	19	29	28	52	20.7	17.7
Hong Kong	18	25	29	100	12.7	9.4
Singapore	25	41	46	196	4.2	12.0
Malaysia	41	26	32	51	6.1	3.8
AVERAGE	21%	23%	24%	24%	5.4%	7.1%
Lower middle- income LDCs						
Indonesia	27%	19%	23%	22%	3.5%	4.4%
Thailand	19	21	21	25	5.2	9.1
Philippines	13	21	29	16	2.3	7.9
Papua New Guinea	40	7	29	36	12.3	23.7
Brunei	21	–	–	113	2.7	47.5
AVERAGE	21%	17%	23%	20%	5.3%	1.6%

SOURCES: World Bank 1984. Data for Taiwan savings and investment ratios are 1981 figures from Kuo 1983: 21. Other Taiwan data are from Republic of China 1984. The figure for Hong Kong central government expenditure is from Hong Kong Government, 1984-85 Budget, statistical tables. Export growth rates for Papua New Guinea and Brunei are from UNCTAD 1983a. Brunei Government expenditure ratio and export ratio are from Far Eastern Economic Review 1984.
[a]Figures for Taiwan, Singapore, Papua New Guinea, and Brunei are for 1970-80.

search to improve techniques. Wider markets allow research costs to be recouped, making research more remunerative; a freer flow of information makes research less expensive. Feedback from international markets provides easier access to information on new methods and products.

Furthermore, international markets stimulate countries to adjust to changing conditions and to handle new opportunities with dexterity. They also improve maneuverability. Thus countries that had deliberately tried to restrict themselves to importing "necessities" found it much harder to adjust to the energy price shock. When the prices of products soared, the inward-looking countries experienced enormous difficulties and cutbacks in the use of their industrial capacity.[22] Imports of the outward-oriented countries, however, needed only temporary reduction, until a surge of new exports covered the increased import bill.

A successful outward-oriented strategy can only be achieved by a decentralized market economy with a rational price structure and adequate macroeconomic stabilization policies. It is likely, however, that an export orientation will further improve the qualities of economic policymaking. Thus there will be indirect as well as direct gains from trade. Not only entrepreneurs but politicians must be more responsive to change. International interdependence will provide rapid feedback on macroeconomic policies. There is of course no guarantee that rapid feedback will prevent the pursuit of erroneous macroeconomic policies. In such cases, the outward orientation will collapse (as has happened in many countries that have undertaken only half-hearted efforts to reverse inward-looking policies).

A liberalization of trade means that entrepreneurs will have to earn a living by production and marketing rather than by culling favors from the government. Better conditions for business also encourage those with entrepreneurial talents into actually becoming entrepreneurs rather than bureaucrats. Fewer authorities to befriend and fewer regulations to unsnarl provide another important advantage. When ordinary production costs allow it, it is easier for entrepreneurs and industrialists to locate themselves outside the megapolis.

It is useful to explore more fully what is meant by an "outward-oriented" or export-promoting strategy. The point is not that it is advantageous to introduce a set of distortions that make it more profitable to export than to produce for the home market. It is certainly possible to waste resources by pushing goods onto the international markets at prices that do not reflect the full sacrifice needed to produce them. An outward orientation implies a redirection of policies away from a previously prevalent strategy of import substitution. Because the advantages of trade go beyond the gains stemming from a reallocation of factors of production, however, export-promoting distortions are preferable to the distortions of costs and incentives resulting from import substitution.

Explanations of high growth among Asian-Pacific countries in terms of economic policies do not have to rely on ad hoc theorizing. They seize upon common characteristics in an otherwise extremely heterogenous region. The economic policy argument has the added strength that it is an extension of analyses of why the West grew rich. In a recent analysis of the economic history of the West, Nathan Rosenberg and L. E. Birdzell explore the development of markets and capitalist institutions and highlight the importance of the evolutionary process fostered by capitalism and its economic freedoms: "The West has grown rich, by comparison to other economies, by allowing its economic sector autonomy to experiment in the development of new and diverse products, methods of manufacture, modes of enterprise organization, market relationships, methods of transportation and communication, and even relationships between capital and labor."[23] Rosenberg and Birdzell stress the function of the market economy not only as an instrument for gathering information about consumers' preferences in order to allocate resources wisely, but also as a device for developing ideas about the most efficient ways to organize economic activity (ways that change constantly as basic conditions change). They argue that the autonomy granted not only to the economic sector but also to the fields of science and technology plays an important role in eliminating political domination and religious and ideological fetters on experimentation. When this freedom to experiment and evolve is extended to both the economic and technological sectors, it is also possible to translate the advances of science into economic innovations. "The whole combination," they say, "is as unique historically as the West's wealth."[24]

The Asian-Pacific countries have imported technologies from the West, and some, like Japan, have improved on them. They have also devised economic systems that permit and encourage not only accumulation and efficiency but experimentation and evolution. There is nothing miraculous about the success of the Asian-Pacific countries. They are all unique, but they have a unifying characteristic. Basically, they have all pursued similar economic policies within the same economic system. To generalize further, this system and these policies are the same as those that brought the established industrial countries their high levels of success—even if some of their present policies and indecisive behavior would seem to belie the fact.

A generalization requires a conscious sacrifice of detail in order to gain the perspective allowed by simplicity. There is no doubt that it would be possible to make a much more complicated analysis of Pacific growth. By focusing on particulars, one could, for instance, explain more about Japanese growth, Korean growth, or Singaporean growth. The more widespread the growth, however, the more likely it is that there is some general explanation and that the particulars provide the detail and the color rather than the structure. This truth holds for the Pacific region, even if there is strong resistance to it among those who venerate "the special case approach" to Hong Kong, Taiwan, or Japan—whether because they have vested interests in the ideology of less successful systems or because they adhere to a "miracle" theory that presupposes specialized knowledge of a particular country.

Some Demonstration Effects on Economic Policy

The success of Japan and the impressive progress made by the Asian NICs and other Pacific countries have had an electrifying effect not only on the Pacific region itself but also on other countries. There has been a demonstration effect on both economic thinking and economic policymaking. The affinity of the policies of the West and the Asian-Pacific region makes it possible to suggest that the Asian-Pacific rise has reminded the established industrial countries of the utility of the system under which they achieved their own prominence.[25] Arguments for the efficiency and virtues of markets and capitalist incentives have been strengthened by research not only into the negative results of regulation at home but also into the positive results of deregulation in Asian-Pacific countries. The following passage from Milton and Rose Friedman may be quoted as an illustration: "In the Far East, Malaysia, Singapore, Korea, Taiwan, Hong Kong, and Japan—all relying extensively on private markets—are thriving. Their people are full of hope. An economic explosion is under way in these countries. . . . The intellectual apologists for centralized economic planning sang the praise of Mao's China until Mao's successors trumpeted China's backwardness and bemoaned the lack of progress during the past twenty-five years."[26]

The rapid recovery and growth of Japan in the postwar period has created an interest in cloning. The Western countries search for messages in the special applications made in Japan. "Japan has become the new reference point for the developing nations and the West, and comparisons with Japan cause increasing wonder and sometimes envy."[27] A growing literature abounds with lessons to be learned from Japan, whether it be in macroeconomic policy, industrial policy, managerial techniques, quality control methods, education, or social welfare policies.[28]

If we turn to the poor countries, we may consider how, long ago, the Meiji Restoration (or revolution) inspired many Asian leaders to make their first movements toward independence and modernization in the prewar period. Japan had been able to adapt and industrialize and, in the process, to build up a modern nation capable of keeping the Western powers at bay. The original international demonstration effect of Japan was profound.[29] The lack of a theoretical foundation to explain the model, however, made the Japanese method of instilling fiber into the people and building an independent nation seem unique and impossible to replicate. In addition, the Japanese example encountered resistance from those violently opposed to the West; for a closer evaluation revealed that, behind the institutional screens, the economics of the restoration were reminiscent of the Western system. Ultimately, Japan's imperialist ambitions undid the Japanese model in the minds of those struggling for freedom and development.

Thus, in spite of the almost intimidating success of the Japanese development strategy, most third world leaders, intent on moving away from colonialism, chose in varying degrees to base their ideals upon socialism and to take their marching orders from communism. The need for comprehensive planning became central to their efforts, and was urged even by the representatives of Western nations where it had never been practiced.

A different process was set in motion by the Japanese postwar rise. By the late 1950's the close neighbors of Japan—frustrated by failure with inward-looking development strategies—were already being stimulated to attempt systematic use of the Japanese model and to achieve a Japanese-style political economy. Korea and Taiwan also had as a model the considerable achievements of Hong Kong, attained under far from favorable conditions. The precedents made it easier for Korea and Taiwan to proceed in a new direction, a direction that, considering the state of development thinking among both theoreticians and practitioners at the time, must have appeared hazardous.

Today, when a whole group of countries with very diverse backgrounds have achieved rapid growth, the model takes on new significance and its influence is becoming increasingly widespread. The Japanese miracle is no longer the only example—depressing in that miracles are hard to duplicate. In the same region there are now also a number of newly industrializing countries to watch, countries in the midst of transformation. The four Asian NICs, with under 2 percent of the total population of the developing world, have almost 7 percent of its GDP, close to 20 percent of its total trade, and nearly 60 percent of its manufactured exports. And there is a leverage effect: socialist setbacks have provided a painful contrast that has directed the attention of those who are disillusioned to the advantages of other systems.

The foregoing analysis of Asian-Pacific growth has focused on the outward orientation and the institutional changes that accompany this strategy. An outward orientation is in agreement with established trade theory. Yet its success caught many observers by surprise. Attempts to accommodate trade theory in the development theories of the 1950's and 1960's had suggested that, at least during an intermediate period, import substitution was the only way to overcome trade difficulties, avoid bottlenecks, and escape from raw-material export traps, and this view was widely accepted. The successful experiences of the newly industrializing countries of Asia—and the contrasting experiences of countries that tried inward-looking strategies—have therefore had a dramatic effect on trade policy thinking. Anne Krueger summarizes the situation well. "The important points are these," she says: "(1) no observer of any of [the NICs] can possibly doubt that the remarkable rates of growth were somehow closely related to factors associated with the rapid growth of exports; (2) for all countries where it is possible to contrast performance before and after policy changes, there could be little doubt that the growth rate jumped sharply after adoption of export-oriented strategies; and (3) the fact that the high growth rates of real GNP were sustained for a very long period of time suggests strongly that the accelerated growth was not due simply to static gains from improved resource allocation." And again: "—From a [trade] theory without any evidence in the early 1960's suggesting departures from free trade for dynamic reasons, the tables are totally turned."[30] In recent years there has been little reasoned opposition to such views. What once were coherent contrary interpretations have collapsed.[31]

The demonstration effect is felt in the trade policy thinking of other developing countries in the Asian-Pacific region. The achievements of the Asian-Pacific NICs are made all the more remarkable by the fact that they seem to be more stable than those of other NICs. No other countries classified by the OECD as NICs—in Southern Europe, Latin America, or Asia— have the same record of success. Considerable differences exist in the policies pursued by the NICs. On balance, the Asian-Pacific NICs have relied less on foreign borrowing, and more on foreign trade, private industry, small scale business, and agriculture than their Latin American counterparts, whose growth has been rapid but shaky.

When other Asian-Pacific countries have shifted, like the NICs, to a greater outward orientation coupled with deregulation, they too have prospered. The success of one group of nations is especially noteworthy. Thailand, Indonesia, Malaysia, and the Philippines all belong to a select group of twelve developing countries that had an even faster rate of growth in manufactured exports during the 1970's than the NICs. Thailand and Indonesia had an annual rate of growth in manufactured exports of 50 percent, Malaysia of 40 percent, and the Philippines of 32 percent. It might be argued that the rapidly growing manufactured exports of these NECs took off from a small base, making subsequent percentage increases appear comparatively large. The performance continued strong all through the decade, however, and even accelerated toward the end of it (when the base was higher and outside circumstances were in many respects more complicated). At the end of the decade, Malaysia and Thailand ranked by far the highest among the NECs in terms of absolute amounts of manufactured exports. Of the twelve new export stars, the Philippines ranked third and Indonesia eighth.[32]

The strategy tried out by the Asian-Pacific countries has attracted attention among policy makers outside the region. In his essay on trade policy for developing countries, Donald Keesing observes that "most officials of developing countries, [like] practically all specialists in economic development, are aware that one can document startling histories of success" in Korea, Taiwan, Singapore, and elsewhere, and that "one can also find many other cases of partial success and failure which either reinforce the same lessons or teach useful supplementary ones." "Perhaps even more important," he continues, "application in new settings of the combination of what is now known and recommended—particularly in countries well along in the process of development—gives very encouraging results, even if it does not usually turn other countries into success stories on the same scale as Korea." Later he notes that the 1970's saw, "in many developing countries, a swing in the views of officials themselves, their economic advisors, many business leaders, and much educated opinion, toward support for pro-trade policies complete with widespread economic reforms."[33]

The empirical evidence of the Pacific record has probably influenced not only attitudes to trade but development policy in general. There is some dissatisfaction with the "poverty of development economics"—to use Deepak Lal's phrase—an approach that tends to overemphasize what governments can achieve by ordering things around.[34] The "laissez-rien-faire" of the LDCs has caused a frustration that may be dispelled by the Asian-Pacific demonstration effect. A paralyzing fascination with outside assistance and planning and a preoccupation with the ills of colonialism are diminishing somewhat in the face of, among other things, the impressive growth achieved by the crown colony of Hong Kong. Hong Kong belies both the theory of exploitation and the notion that take-off requires aid. Hong Kong has received, not billions in aid, but millions in refugees from a different economic system. There is now a noticeable increase in scepticism about the effectiveness of international aid, in part because of such demonstrations that there are other paths to economic growth. The advantages of receiving aid may, after all, be outweighed by the disadvantages of the "learned helplessness" it produces.[35]

Asian-Pacific growth is likely to affect the North-South dialogue. Even the most successful Asian-Pacific countries have a weak voice in the affairs of the LDCs. They are all small, and Hong Kong and Taiwan have the peculiar international problems of non-countries. Continued progress in Southeast Asia, however, and continued cooperation among the ASEAN nations, will help raise their influence to a level that better accords with their achievements.

Among the LDCs and in the discussions between the Group of 77—the forum of the developing countries—and the industrial nations ("Group B"), ASEAN representatives have taken intermediate positions, reflecting not just diplomatic efforts but different real interests. The ASEAN economist Amado Castro comments that, "in the Group of 77, ASEAN is perceived as a moderate grouping and now both the Group of 77 and the Group B countries are looking to ASEAN for leadership in bridging various positions."[36] We may also recall a point made in the Ohira Report, which finds it noteworthy that "the developing countries of the region are maintaining a moderate and realistic stance in the North-South dialogue. The chance is great that the region as a whole will be a model for developing a new pattern in North-South relations."[37]

The Asian-Pacific countries have different concerns from those that have dominated the North-South dialogue—or rather the angry monologue of the South. A strong demonstration effect will change Southern diplomacy. The East Asian countries have demonstrated that it is not necessary to wait passively for gifts, and that it is possible to take active steps to grow and become efficient. They have shown that there is an alternative to degrading demands for favors. In their view, the protectionism of established countries should not be facilitated by a downplaying of the gains from trade by the newly successful countries. Rather, the industrial countries should be pressured to keep open, and not block with trade obstacles, the road to progress they themselves have already traveled successfully.

Economic Reform in China

If China is influenced by its neighbors to institute reforms and enter the international economy, the Asian-Pacific demonstration effect will be highlighted. Because of China's prestige, the power of the demonstration effect would be greatly strengthened in the socialist South and the communist East. The effects on world politics and world economics would be significant. China is already engaged in a considerable effort to reform its economic system. Maoist radicalism has been explicitly rejected. Soviet planning has been eased. Stalinist concentration on massive, capital-intensive investments has been discontinued. Yet the reform movement so far has proceeded along (reinterpreted) Marxist lines. Carefully legitimized, and in no way characterized as a tacit surrender of communism, it has been far-reaching. In 1984 Harry Harding described the situation as follows: "Ever since the death of Mao Zedong in October, 1976—and especially since Deng Xiaoping's rise to preeminence in December of 1978—China has experienced a period of almost unprecedented dynamism. Virtually every institution in the country . . . has undergone thorough reexamination and extensive change. The

China of the 1970's has been transformed almost beyond recognition."[38] Even since these words were written, the reform movement has advanced considerably.

To what extent, if any, has growth among the capitalist countries of the Asian-Pacific region influenced and stimulated the Chinese reform movement? Like some East European countries, China had already experimented with economic reforms before Pacific dynamism could have had much impact. Present reform efforts, however, are more ambitious and persistent. Asian-Pacific dynamism may well have a bearing upon this intensification. Reforms may be triggered because of economic difficulties and dissatisfactions—because economic performance is not up to domestic expectations. "Economic difficulties," however, are usually relative; they are perceived as such in the light of what is achieved elsewhere. The economic standard has long been set by the Western nations. But for China there is now a new, nearer, and more imposing yardstick: the Asian-Pacific countries and their accomplishments. The Chinese must feel a temptation to do something dramatic to avoid slipping into giant insignificance and providing a reverse of the demonstration effect, an example of how things should not be done.

Like the Soviet Union, China has a large domestic market. The pressures to abandon inward-looking planning are therefore less intense for China than for the smaller East European countries with their more limited domestic markets. Reform pressures might also be expected to be less intense in China than in the Soviet Union, since the Chinese revolution is more recent and economic aspirations have not been frustrated for so many years. Yet there has been a more determined economic reform movement in China than in the Soviet Union itself and most of the Soviet Union's smaller East European satellites. The situation of China differs from that of the Soviet Union in that the Soviet leaders do not have the example of neighboring countries where members of their own ethnic group do exceedingly well under capitalism, even in the most difficult circumstances. For Soviet ideologues and politicians the search for explanations of domestic problems may be less troubling than for the Chinese, who cannot ignore the economic rise of their countrymen in Taiwan, Singapore, and Hong Kong. They must wonder. They must also contemplate the Chinese diaspora in Southeast Asia and its success under a different economic system. The historical closeness between the motherland and the overseas Chinese strengthens these impressions.

Such comparisons may be expected to provoke reforms in China, and they have. The question is whether these reforms are not only triggered but also given content and structure by the examples from neighboring countries. A definite answer is hard to provide. In the literature on Chinese economic reforms I find no discussion of the question.[39] Indeed, no attention seems to be paid to the phenomenon of Asian-Pacific success as a yardstick and a challenge. This is all the more surprising since the hypotheses suggest themselves so easily. But invariably I hear it argued, in conversations with people in Asian-Pacific countries in a position to know, that the Chinese have undoubtedly been influenced both by the progress of their neighbors and by the way this progress has been achieved. The reflections of the Chinese leaders and thinkers may be rendered less painful if they can tell themselves that what is being carried out in the Asian-Pacific neighborhood is something different from classic Western capitalism. Even so, none of them would freely admit that they are furtively watching.

That China has been influenced by the success records of neighboring countries is not easy to ascertain from Chinese writings. Given the limited room for discussion in China, it should not be expected that influential people would put themselves enthusiastically on record on such topics; they could all too easily be represented—now or later—as "capi-

talist reform mongers."[40] Their silence makes it hard to sub-
stantiate the workings of the demonstration effect on China.
But it is far from being proof that there is no such effect. To
find traces of the demonstration effect, it is necessary to do
some reading between the lines. As Chalmers Johnson has observed, there are hints in Chinese sources, and in reports on
them, that "since the death of Mao Tse-tung even China has
come to acknowledge, if not yet emulate, the achievements of
the capitalist developmental state."[41] Davie and Carver make
a similar observation in connection with the Chinese rethink-
ing of their export policies in 1979: "Articles in the Chinese
press extolled the virtues of the economies of Japan, South
Korea, and Taiwan—countries which developed through promotion of export industries. Chinese economists called for
the country to specialize along the lines of comparative advantage—in labor-intensive industries—in order to maximize
the gains from trade."[42]

There have also been some interesting changes in the research agenda of the Center of Japanese Studies of the important Academy of Social Sciences, a government think tank in
Beijing. Work at the Center has been redirected from more
propagandistic and derogatory discussions of topics like the
roots of Japanese fascism to serious analyses of the political
economy of Japan and the consequences and the lessons of
rapid Japanese growth for other countries. According to Zhou
Bin, the two questions about Japan that interest Chinese
researchers most are: (1) What were the driving forces behind
Japan's postwar era of rapid economic growth—and what
strengths and methods enabled the Japanese to rise out of
total desolation to restore their nation and build it into the
economic giant we see today? and (2) How has Japan, a part
of Asia like China and India, been able to achieve a higher
level of economic development than those two ancient cultures, which have larger populations, vast land areas, and

bountiful resources?[43] With respect to Japan, Richard Nanto has also observed that "China's four modernizations, by which it plans to develop during the last two decades of the twentieth century, are reminiscent of Japan's thrust for 'fukoku kyo-hei' (rich nation, strong military) during the late nineteenth century."[44]

Taiwan's success has also been acknowledged. Yu Qiu-li, a high-ranking Chinese official, had this to say in a speech on "political economic relationships": "There is nothing wrong with a cabinet being an economic cabinet rather than a political cabinet. If people criticize that—let them. Chiang Ching Kou [the President of Taiwan] has gathered around him a group of economists to run the Taiwan Economic Cabinet. In my view there is nothing wrong with that. Taiwan's economy has grown very rapidly. The general living standard of the people there is several times higher than that of our people in the provinces. Its national income is said to rank 44th in the world, and Taiwan has been included in the richer areas. It would not do any harm to learn from this economic cabinet. It is easy to speak of one's own achievements; to have an enemy say anything good of you is not easy. I wonder whether you people [the audience] have thought of that."[45]

The Chinese are surely aware of the success of neighboring countries. They throw furtive glances at it and ponder the conclusions to draw from it. Seymour Martin Lipset reports the following on the basis of wide discussions in China during a lecture tour in May-June 1984: "There were occasional references to what some called the four young tigers, namely Hong Kong, Singapore, Taiwan, and South Korea. The Chinese are aware that all of these countries are doing well, and they take a certain amount of pride in this, as well as a certain amount of security, in that they see these four areas as demonstrating the compatibility of Chinese culture with economic development and modernization. No one spoke to me about the politics of Taiwan. On the rare occasions on which Taiwan was mentioned in passing, the reference reflected or pertained to Taiwan's economic growth and prosperity."[46]

Undoubtedly, the economic reforms in China are to some extent an attempt to make China's performance better match the performance of some of its neighbors. It is also likely that the content of some of the reforms is inspired by those examples. This is not to say that the Chinese are plagiarizing. Huan Hsiang, Vice President of the Academy of Social Sciences, has perhaps provided the best summing up of the situation: "While our nation's economy is already very objective . . . the comrades at the Social Science Institute still bring up the issue of Asia's 'four small tigers,' which are Taiwan, Hong Kong, South Korea, and Singapore. Can they be taken as models? . . . After thorough study, it has been decided that China can in no way follow such models. . . . We cannot blindly plagiarize from foreign economic models when implementing economic reforms."[47]

Some of the reform pressures result from foreign trade. All the communist countries engage in international trade to take advantage of some of the benefits of specialization and to rectify shortages, gaps, and surpluses caused by inward-looking planning. To a large extent this trade is conducted among the communist countries themselves. But this "second world market"—to use a communist description—has not proved versatile enough to make trade with the capitalist world unnecessary. For China, the impulse to trade with outsiders has been stronger than for other communist countries. The example set by neighboring countries has included a demonstration of the importance of international trade. Geographical reasons have also made these countries more of an ersatz market for China then they would otherwise have been. Consequently, there has been a rapid decline in Chinese exports to the communist countries. In 1960 they constituted 60 percent of total exports, but by 1983 they had declined to no more than 3 percent, a remarkably low figure compared with those for other communist countries. For instance, Soviet exports to other communist countries in 1982 made up almost 50 percent of total Soviet exports.[48]

If the market economies, eager to export, have willingly tried to adjust to Chinese ways of doing things, the Chinese, eager to get their own trade under way, have needed to adjust to some of the institutional characteristics of the market economies. The importance historically attributed by China to the Chinese diaspora has facilitated this process. *Far Eastern Economic Review* of November 22, 1984, has a cover story about the "call of the motherland" and the way "China uses patriotism to encourage the support of its overseas sons."

China's special ties with Hong Kong have long been important in transmitting the economic lessons, and the constitutional predicament of Hong Kong, passing from British rule to Chinese sovereignty in 1997, strengthens this importance. China reaps significant economic gains from its trade and other economic contacts with Hong Kong, and there should be some attraction in at least preserving–if not expanding–these gains. Moreover, there is a desire not to make the Formosa straits wider and deeper by turning Hong Kong into a ruin. The interest China has in finding a way to accommodate the Hong Kong of 1997, and to set out the future rules of the game now, adds yet another dimension to the workings of the demonstration effect. Beijing must reflect on what it is that makes (and what it will take to make) Hong Kong function. In the process, new insights may be gained–adding to the demonstration effect and the reform momentum. Perhaps China has imported that Asian-Pacific capitalist institution, "the special economic zone," in an effort to facilitate–inconspicuously–a Hong Kong solution. In the process, it is developing a mechanism that will allow the demonstration effect freer play on a regional basis in China itself.[49]

The implications of the situation in Hong Kong are far-reaching, as is made clear by the agreement of September 1984 between the United Kingdom and China. Although the agreement accords Hong Kong many freedoms, it also leaves many questions unresolved. The future of the colony will depend on how the agreement is interpreted, implemented, and respected. A reformist China government would have fewer qualms about letting Hong Kong continue on its present course. The optimist might add that a China in an antireform mood would have stronger reasons to leave open the economic window afforded by Hong Kong. (After all, it was kept open even during the Cultural Revolution.) Yet nagging questions and pessimistic speculations abound. A Hong Kong that probably could function better with no government at all may prove unmanageable by a hypergovernment—even if that government does its best not to be a bull in the store of China.

The extraordinary attractions and special features of Hong Kong would be difficult for even a country with a capitalist track record to take over. Things that would be hard for most Western governments to handle would probably be even harder for the communists. For example, banks in capitalist countries may not find it attractive to carry out a substantial part of their operations in a place that will be part of a communist country. Communist sovereignty may prove even more problematical for Hong Kong's Asian banking and financial business, much of which is predicated on the colony's reputation as a haven of discretion. There is also a vitally important competition among the Asian-Pacific countries—as there is between all countries—to offer attractive living and working conditions. Uncertainty about the future rules of the game for Hong Kong casts shadows over investors' confidence there. In view of the difficulties looming over the colony, other countries have already made efforts to offer the Hong Kong services—with a view to attracting, not least from Hong Kong itself, both talent and capital.[50] In sum, it is not going to be easy for China to swallow Hong Kong without chewing it up–and it would be a great setback to the Asian-Pacific region and beyond if Hong Kong were to go down in history as an "Atlantis of the Pacific."

China is no monolith. There is an ongoing discussion and controversy and there can be dramatic changes and turnabouts. For the reforms to be efficient and successful, there must be a reasonably rational price structure to guide decentralized decision making, and this condition may not be met. Reform failures will invite vigorous opposition. The ideologues, the planning bureaucracy, and those enjoying special privileges under a Soviet-type system resent reforms; and among the military there are probably many who by virtue of their training do not readily sympathize with the idea of letting the "chaos of the market" guide the "long march" they would prefer to command.

These currents and countercurrents are reflected in an article in *Far Eastern Economic Review* regarding the Japanese visit of Hu Yaobang, Secretary General of the Chinese Communist Party, in November 1983. The article is also interesting as an indication of the demonstration effect at work: "Greater intimacy with the Japanese leaders will enable Hu to give stronger support to Zhao and his economic reforms. The 'open door' policy toward trade and technical exchange has come under fire recently from Maoist-conservative elements in the party and the People's Liberation Army on the grounds that it means importing 'spiritual' pollution from the advanced countries with their 'decadent' morals. Hu will be better equipped to confront such criticism after he has seen Japan and–it is to be hoped–other capitalist countries." [51]

Whether or not decentralization measures in China can be legitimized in Marxist terms, any economically successful reforms will necessitate the creation of pluralistic power centers and the consequent loss of some party control. This will not be suffered gladly by the guardians of Marxist policy. The conflicts between economic needs and party creeds in China have the potential to set in motion violent shifts in policy and ideology.

Whatever the future developments in China, they will be of monumental importance to the position of the Pacific region in world affairs. The economic gravity shift will be given considerable impetus if China's reforms increase the efficiency of its economic system and bring the country into closer contact with its neighbors and their economic system.

The Decline of Socialist Influence

The reform movement in China is a manifestation of the power of the demonstration effect and of the political challenge it represents to the adherents of a socialist economic system. Even if the movement suffers severe reverses, the present reform activities and the prospect of their success have already jolted the Soviet Union at least as dramatically as the defection of China from the Soviet fold once did. Perhaps the ideological defection is the more serious blow, since it goes beyond the historical animosity between the two countries, and constitutes a blow to Soviet self-image.

There is a rivalry between the Atlantic and the Pacific, too, but it is being played out within what is basically the same economic system. It has a totally different basis from the competition taking place between the Asian-Pacific countries and the socialist world. The latter is an encounter, not within a system, but *between* systems. It is a "high ec" rivalry, more striking than the "high tech" race (or at least fateful in a different way).

Japan is deepening the wound to Marxism that was inflicted by the United States and the other industrial countries when they failed to bear out Marx's predictions of the collapse of capitalism. Marx originally held that capitalism in its initial phase was an effective engine of growth. In the opening pages of the Communist Manifesto, he states that the bourgeoisie (the class of modern capitalists) "has been the first to show what man's activity can bring about. It has accomplished wonders far surpassing Egyptian pyramids, Roman aqueducts, and Gothic cathedrals; it has conducted expeditions that put in the shade all former exoduses of nations and crusades. . . . The bourgeoisie, by the rapid improvement of all instruments of production, by the immensely facilitated means of communication, draws all, even the most barbarian, nations into civilization. The cheap prices of its commodities are the heavy artillery with which it batters down all Chinese walls." Marx had no difficulty in making these seemingly generous acknowledgments, since the inherent contradictions in the very achievements of the bourgeoisie contained, he thought, the seeds of their own destruction.

The increasing prosperity of the "capitalists," however, yielded increasing wealth for the "proletariat" instead of the increasing misery Marx had foretold; and it continued to do so. This was troubling to Marx himself, and it has been increasingly troubling to his followers. Some saving argument had to be found. The neo-Marxists cannot afford Marx's largesse. They do not recognize even a passing constructiveness in capitalism. The capitalist states had risen and survived, they argue, only by taking unfair advantage of the rest of the world and by passing on a small part of its loot to their own working class. The neo-Marxist school of thought in development economics therefore attributes the poverty of third world nations to the effects of capitalism radiating from the center to the periphery.

Paul Baran is perhaps the best-known representative of this approach. "Far from serving as an engine of economic expansion, of technological progress, and of social change," he argues, "the capitalist order in these countries has represented a framework for economic stagnation, for archaic technology, and for social backwardness." "It is in the underdeveloped world," he contends, "that the central, overriding fact of our epoch becomes manifest to the naked eye: the capitalist system, once a mighty engine of economic development, has turned into a no less formidable hurdle to human advancement." [52]

The success of the Asian-Pacific countries has proved otherwise. As Ian Little points out, Baran had no way of foreseeing that, "in East Asia, capitalism would produce results that make its nineteenth-century performance look like that of a donkey." [53] The Asian NICs are delivering a second shock to Marxism. Not only does it remain clear that, contrary to what Marx claimed, advanced capitalism can avoid disintegration; it has also been demonstrated that, contrary to the neo-Marxists' claim, newcomers can rise by means of capitalism. In the 1950's and early 1960's the principal contenders were thought to be India, with its democratic socialism, and China, with its totalitarian communism. The disillusionment suffered by these celebrated contestants now heightens their interest—and that of other countries—in the model practiced by long-unnoticed newcomers who are presently taking an unexpected and commanding lead. The Marxist (and the socialist) methods have accordingly lost their attraction—even, it seems, among many of their own practitioners. Thus the lessons of Asian-Pacific success have precipitated an enormous economic and political change.

Radical critiques employing concepts like "periphery," "dependency," "exploitation," and "delinking" have lost much of their previous attraction. The examples of the Pacific countries have demonstrated their irrelevance as analytical tools. Korea, Taiwan, Singapore, and in particular Hong Kong—a colony—have played havoc with neo-Marxist views of the world; the subdued practitioners of these views capture few headlines nowadays. The tenets of the less doctrinaire socialists have also been shaken. It is hardly surprising that the success of the NICs is widely resented. As the facts of Asian-Pacific growth become highlighted over a longer and longer period, Marxist speculations—repeated so often that they have begun to sound like truths—will be increasingly difficult to uphold. It will no longer be possible to view things only in terms of vicious cycles of poverty, exploitation through trade, a secular fall in the terms of trade, irreparable damages from colonialism, the necessity of massive transfers, the importance of controls, regulations, and planning, and the vagaries and injustices of the market mechanism.[54]

The decline in the intellectual power of neo-Marxist and socialist doctrines is paralleled by the shrinking political influence of their practitioners. The relative stagnation of the communist countries in comparison with the Asian-Pacific nations poses political problems for the Soviet Union in particular. At the same time as the communists' resource base has been slowly expanding, their political ties with the Asian-Pacific countries have been loosened. The masses of Asia and the less-developed world are looking in a different direction, and communist hardware and socialist software are less in vogue. Countries that still subscribe to rigid planning are witnessing the shadow of starvation rather than the glow of emerging affluence. The pragmatists experiment with economic reforms, and are watched with suspicion by the ideologues.

In spite of a considerable build-up of naval and air power in the Asian-Pacific region, Soviet influence there has been gradually declining. As Donald Zagoria notes: "Ideologically . . . pro-Soviet, Marxist forces in East Asia are increasingly on the defensive. The strength of indigenous communist and Marxist forces in East Asia is considerably less today than at any time since the end of World War II." Zagoria continues with further examples of the wane of Soviet influence in the region: "The Japanese Socialist party has suffered a substantial decline in popular votes throughout most of the 1970's. . . . The new Chinese leaders have adopted a bold new pragmatic course of economic development that includes many 'capitalist' devices. . . . In Indonesia, Thailand, and Malaysia, where a decade or two ago communist parties were serious contenders for power, they are no longer so."[55] Robert Scalapino makes similar observations: "From the perspective of the early 1980's, the Soviet Union would be justified in regarding the early 1950's as its golden age in Asia. . . . The USSR's political relations with most other countries of East Asia have remained static or deteriorated, and with a few exceptions, influence over the Asian communist parties is now negligible. . . . In sum . . . the USSR's political and economic position has experienced an overall decline in the Pacific-Asian area during the past three decades."[56]

In Asia, where according to Khrushchev the world battle for the masses was to be won, the position of communism has deteriorated sharply. Even when domestic political problems are serious, as in the Philippines, for instance, the domino theory is now rarely invoked for East Asia. There are still apprehensions about the possibility of attack and subversion, but not the same kinds of anxieties there once were. Neighbors cannot so easily export subversion when it is demonstrable that they have only misery to offer. It is widely accepted that, short of open aggression, expansionist foreign policies are not capable of making countries fall like ninepins.[57]

Among the late-developing countries of the world, it is possible to distinguish different social classes. The "proletariat," or poorest countries, are a group made up primarily of countries that have adopted socialist methods of development. At the other extreme, the "landed gentry" are composed of countries rich from the rents of great natural resources, especially oil. In between, there is an emerging third class—the "bourgeoisie," or middle class—made up primarily of the Asian-Pacific countries. These countries have managed to industrialize, use their economic resources efficiently, and make a spectacular entry into world markets. Their success is founded on market economies that permit and encourage evolution. If serious constraints are placed on the demonstration effect, the Third World will grow apart. If, instead, the demonstration effect is allowed free rein, greater numbers will join this middle class, enabling it to replay the historical role played by the middle class within the established industrial countries— in particular, to demonstrate that social and economic mobility can produce prosperity better than class struggle, and without the bloodshed.

Limits to the Demonstration Effect

Admittedly, there are many obstacles to the workings of the demonstration effect. But it should not be concluded that there is no such effect just because not everyone is converted and not every country has altered its policies. First of all, facts are often not accepted as facts, and they are usually open to more than one interpretation. As we have seen, there are a good number of "special" explanations of rapid Asian-Pacific growth. They still have their adherents even though they were more persuasive when they were required to illuminate just one or two "miracles" rather than to explain why, under certain conditions, so many miracles seem to occur.

Another obstacle to the demonstration effect is a strong and diffused disbelief in the market mechanism and a resistance to surrendering to its apparent vagaries. Markets certainly do suffer from insufficiencies and inefficiencies, and these have inspired a multiplicity of corrective political interventions. The industrially advanced nations have only recently realized that the costs of failed political interventions often far outweigh the costs of market failures. In many developing countries, heavy regulations have distorted the signals, causing a highly visible, socially unproductive, and unscrupulous competition for rents. In these cases, there will be deep-seated misunderstandings of the workings of markets and the role of regulators. The market mechanism has in many instances been discredited because it has been propagating the signals of the regulators.

Another problem is that the regulators themselves, who thrive on controls, will often oppose an open-market policy. Politicians and bureaucrats (even solidly honest ones) have an interest in preserving systems that make them appear engaged and active. Decentralizing the markets might be perceived, at least in the short term, as indifference. Of course, the resistance of those who actually know how to profit from the dispensations of the regulators will be encountered everywhere. What results is a strange and powerful alliance between profiteers and idealists—between those who see merits in regulations and those who see profits in exploiting them.[58]

Different value judgements also explain why Asian-Pacific growth is not universally appreciated. Ideological inhibitions create a strong resistance to the idea that the Asian NICs have engaged in a spectacular growth process. Long-standing controversies will not be quickly settled by a few Japans, Hong Kongs, and Taiwans—even if the economic policies of these countries are demonstrably the same as those of all countries that have achieved high standards of living. Thus there are many different reactions to Asian-Pacific growth. It is sometimes denied, sometimes denigrated, sometimes looked upon as a special case, and sometimes hailed as a miracle. The growth of the Asian NICs has often been disregarded by those who have been surprised (sometimes unpleasantly so) that that kind of growth is possible. Hong Kong has even been accused of having achieved no real growth, or at least no good growth. And this in spite of the fact that Hong Kong has managed, in the most difficult and hazardous circumstances imaginable, to raise the living standards of its population to European levels. This success is all the more remarkable considering that many of the inhabitants are postwar refugees from countries with different economic systems. In Hong Kong they have been able to achieve a rapidly improving standard of living within a framework of economic freedoms.

The "special case" argument draws no universal lesson and thus serves only the purpose of the particular theorist. To give just one example of this approach, Paul Streeten has argued that there are four special reasons for Taiwanese growth: the Japanese growth pole was so near; there were both indigenous and immigrant entrepreneurs; Taiwan was given favorable trade treatment; and the Vietnam war created a boom economy.[59] Yet one can just as easily offer some altogether contrary "special arguments": the Nationalists who fled to Taiwan in 1949 were demoralized by their defeat; they were hated by the Taiwanese, who outnumbered them almost eight to one; the Japanese-built cities and industries lay in smoldering ruins from Allied bombings; and the withdrawal of Japanese managers and technicians made the rebuilding and operating of factories highly problematic. Comparing the starting points of China and Taiwan, Ramon Myers concludes: "By all accounts the Communist party should have succeeded in building a modern state within a generation and the Nationalist party should have failed and disappeared into history. Initial conditions favored the Communists, not the Nationalists."[60] In reality, there are no special cases. As Ian Little notes, the success of the Asian-Pacific NICs "is almost entirely due to good policies and the ability of the people—scarcely at all to favorable circumstances or a good start."[61]

Because Asian-Pacific growth is resented in many quarters, it is often viewed in a distorted light, even though the facts suggest that, in terms of living standards and a respect for basic human rights, the Asian LDCs typically do far better than countries experimenting with other economic systems and development strategies. In particular, the Asian NICs are frequently accused of pursuing economic growth at the expense of fairness in income distribution—an allegation whose potential to limit the demonstration effect is such that a consideration of the true facts becomes imperative.

It is difficult to formulate a norm that permits comparisons of income distributions. Even given the same income averages, different criteria could be applied to an evaluation of income distributions. Furthermore, it is more than just a methodological problem to determine how much inequality might be compensated for by a higher absolute income level among the poorest inhabitants of a relatively affluent country, or how much initial inequality is acceptable in order to achieve a more equitable income distribution in the future. Income inequalities caused by rewards accruing to power and privilege are likely to reduce growth, but income inequalities that act as strong incentives to work, frugality, and enterprise may well be the positive side of a seemingly unfair growth strategy. Since redistribution of income and reduction of poverty do not necessarily amount to the same thing, the problem is complex. Some studies conclude that the initial phase of a developing country's economic growth may well entail a worsening of income disparities.[62] This may be particularly true of the disparities between urban and rural areas. Yet even by very egalitarian welfare standards, such a growth phase may be considered good; not only does it raise the absolute economic level of the poorest sector of the population, but it may help to usher in a later phase of growth in which income distribution becomes more equitable.

What makes the accusation that the Asian NICs are indifferent to the poor seem strangely misplaced is that these countries have done well on all of three possible scores: (1) by rapid economic growth they have managed to raise the absolute income of their poorest citizens to a level undreamed of by most LDCs; (2) they have achieved more equitable income distributions than most other developing countries; and (3) in spite of occasional reversals of the trend (notably in Korea in the late 1970's), the Asian NICs have typically succeeded in actually lessening disparities in income during the opening phase of their economic growth—something that was formerly thought to be impossible.

The World Bank's *World Development Report* publishes data on income distribution in a number of countries. The data should be used with caution, but they do suggest that Korea and Hong Kong—the two Asian NICs for which estimates are provided by the World Bank—have a more equal income distribution than the other 25 LDCs listed, with the exception of Bangladesh, Yugoslavia, Israel, and perhaps Sri Lanka.[63] Estimates given for Asian-Pacific countries are reproduced in Table 7, together with comparative data for other countries.

Although the Hong Kong authorities have not engaged in rhetoric about income distribution to the same extent as the leaders of India and other countries, income distribution in Hong Kong is more egalitarian and the rise in average income much more rapid. Pronouncements are no substitute for growth and for growth policies that actually improve the situation of the poor.[64] A recent study of income distribution changes in Singapore, for the period 1966-75, concludes that in Singapore, too, there has been rapid growth in average income and an improvement in income distribution.[65]

Taiwan is officially "nonexistent," but many studies have used the good Taiwanese statistics available on household incomes to investigate income distribution and changes in this distribution.[66] The statistics show that income distribution in Taiwan is more egalitarian than in all the countries for which the World Bank provides estimates—and surely most other countries too, whether developed or underdeveloped, and certainly including China. The same conclusion may be drawn about income distribution in Japan.

The communist countries do not provide income distribution statistics. There have been attempts, however, to make

TABLE 7

Income Distribution in Asian-Pacific and Other Countries, Selected Years, 1969-1980

(percentage share of household income by household percentile groups)

Country/Year	Quintile					Highest decile
	Lowest	Second	Third	Fourth	Highest	
Japan, 1979	8.7%	13.2%	17.5%	23.1%	36.8%	21.2%
Korea, 1976	5.7	11.2	15.4	22.4	45.3	27.5
Hong Kong, 1980	5.4	10.8	15.2	21.6	47.0	31.3
Taiwan, 1980	8.8	13.9	17.7	22.8	36.8	—
Indonesia, 1976	6.6	7.8	12.6	23.6	49.4	34.0
Thailand, 1975-76	5.6	9.6	13.9	21.1	49.8	34.1
Philippines, 1970-71	5.2	9.0	12.8	19.0	54.0	38.5
Malaysia, 1973	3.5	7.7	12.4	20.3	56.1	39.8
Australia, 1975-76	5.4	10.0	15.0	22.5	47.1	30.5
Tanzania, 1969	5.8	10.2	13.9	19.7	50.4	35.6
Kenya, 1976	2.6	6.3	11.5	19.2	60.4	45.8
Bangladesh, 1973-74	6.9	11.3	16.1	23.5	42.2	27.4
India, 1975-76	7.0	9.2	13.9	20.5	49.4	33.6
Sri Lanka, 1969-70	7.5	11.7	15.7	21.7	43.4	28.2
United Kingdom, 1979	7.0	11.5	17.0	24.8	39.7	23.4
United States, 1978	4.6	8.9	14.1	22.1	50.3	33.4
Sweden, 1979	7.2	12.8	17.4	25.4	37.2	21.2

SOURCES: World Bank 1984: Table 28, pp. 272-73. For Taiwan, Kuo 1983: Table 6.1, pp. 96-97.

estimates for China. In a recent evaluation of the available empirical material, Thomas Rawski has concluded that the income share of the poorest quintile of the population may have been lower in 1978 than in the 1930's: "Our preliminary survey shows that despite some progress, important features of China's income distribution have not improved significantly since the 1950's or even the 1930's"—this in spite of an impressive array of equity-oriented policies. Rawski speculates that the failures are the unintended consequences of a number of other policies. He points out, for instance, that since there are severe limits on labor mobility, Chinese farmers are not allowed to migrate either to more attractive agricultural communities or to urban areas. The inhabitants of China's poorest regions therefore suffer an unusual degree of continuing impoverishment. He also notes that "there is no reason to believe that China's distributive performance can match the unusual achievements reported for Korea and Taiwan." Rawski's conclusions are supported by other studies too.[67]

The World Bank also offers data on life expectancies and child death rates, which are a good indication of social welfare levels. Hong Kong and Singapore are at the level of industrial market economies; Taiwan is just below this level, and Korea is close to it. These are noteworthy facts if one recalls the criticism often voiced in Western Europe about Asian NICs' lack of involvement in social welfare policies. But social systems differ. That the social systems of the East Asian countries are not all government-controlled and government-financed does not mean that social relations and problems are ignored. There is a tendency in the European welfare states to see the state as the sole source of social welfare. In the East Asian countries there is typically an emphasis on other, nongovernmental welfare networks. For instance, high household savings provide considerable economic security, and strong multigenerational family ties are an additional source of both economic and emotional support. The social problems in a welfare state with high government expenditures on social programs may well exceed those of an East Asian country. Both Japan and the Asian NICs are naturally apprehensive about certain failures of the Western-type welfare states.[68]

Vested interests, politics, and ideology are not the only factors that constrain the demonstration effect. Definite economic difficulties beset the transition from one economic policy regime to another. Factors of production do not flow freely. It takes time to undo distortions. Entrepreneurs are unwilling to commit themselves to export activities until they can be sure that the rules of the game will not soon change again. When distortions are severe and pressures for change more pronounced, vested interests (and political problems) are correspondingly stronger, and beliefs in the permanence of policy changes are weaker.

To further complicate the problems of transition, direct or indirect dismantling of protection systems (for instance, using export subsidies to attract productive resources to export industries and away from import substitution) will stimulate an immediate increase in imports. Since a response to the new export opportunities takes time, there will be a temporary drain on foreign exchange reserves. The management of the changeover is complicated. Economic history is replete with examples of countries that have tried to reorient their trade policies, only to go back later to the previous protectionism. To help reduce the problem of an initial outflow of foreign exchange, the World Bank has introduced so-called "structural adjustment loans." Because structural adjustment is only one of a number of adjustment problems, these loans have sometimes been extended even in the absence of an actual policy reorientation.[69]

Another more economic constraint on the demonstration effect is the increasing protectionism of the industrial countries. Although widespread "trade policy pessimism" is retreating as a result of the Asian-Pacific example, a new "export pessimism" is advancing. Increasingly it is held that protectionism and stagnation will deny newcomers the opportunity to succeed, an argument that finds support in the view that the limited markets of the advanced countries cannot accommodate inundations of goods from more than a few of the developing nations. There would be unfavorable changes in the terms of trade for the new countries and insuperable adjustment problems for the established countries.[70]

Protectionism and slow growth in the industrial countries do pose considerable obstacles. In its *Development Report* for 1984, the World Bank presents some ten-year growth projections for the developing countries; different scenarios are specified depending on growth rates and trade policies in the industrial countries. The protectionist problems, though real, have nevertheless been exaggerated by those unwilling, for reasons of political convenience or ideology, to reorient policies. The LDCs supply a small portion of the total imports of the advanced countries, and make up an even smaller part of the total market for these countries.[71] The problem of protectionism is limited to a number of product lines for which import penetration ratios have become substantial.

Various studies also indicate that, with continued growth, trade patterns become increasingly characterized by intraindustry, or two-way, trade—that is, countries both import and export goods within the same product categories (even at the disaggregated SITC three-digit level). The same changes can be seen in the trade pattern of developing countries.[72] It follows that protectionist pressures are unlikely to grow in proportion to the number of export-oriented LDCs. As some of the successful LDCs continue to grow, they will invest in new, less vulnerable exports, and they will have difficulty in maintaining their export shares in some of the traditional goods, such as textiles. They will have to yield this "one-way trade territory" to newcomers. The net result will be better market opportunities and less severe protectionist barriers for the next generation of NICs than would otherwise be likely. The NICs would already have had to yield a much greater share in traditional LDC exports if it were not for the advantageous quotas alloted them as firstcomers by the protectionist regimes of the established industrial countries. Moreover, in assessing the trade and development strategy one should not forget the record of the "NECs," which during the difficult 1970's managed to increase their exports of manufactured goods to the industrial countries at an even faster rate than the NICs.

Recent research has also shown—and again, this follows

from the tendency toward intraindustry trade—that export opportunities are not tied to growth of total markets in the industrial countries as is sometimes implied. The developing countries often produce close substitutes for manufactured goods made in developed countries. Since the LDCs have a low market share, there should be wide opportunities to capture markets. In these circumstances, says James Riedel, "LDC export growth may be judged to depend less on growth of the market than on the capacity of LDCs to supply manufactured exports at competitive prices."[73]

Finally, in assessing the total trade possibilities for LDCs, one should not forget the opportunities to increase intra-regional trade among the LDCs themselves. The NICs add to the total market for newcomers. By facilitating a more outward orientation in the total LDC group, the LDCs could themselves increase the scope for specialization and trading advantages.[74]

The foregoing considerations notwithstanding, protectionism and the resulting stagnation in the industrial countries do constitute obstacles—needless obstacles but none the less serious in that they derive from facile misunderstandings and even willful misrepresentations. The industrial countries are paying, and exacting, a heavy price in missed opportunities and foregone development. Even worse, they are encouraging developing countries to continue inward-looking strategies based on hostility and suspicion. The United States in particular seems to be doing its best to lose a cold war that has already been won. A recent issue of the *Economist* argued (December 15, 1984) that "if the United States were to permit free trade from Central America, it could create a cluster of thriving Hong Kongs, instead of nests of Sandinistas, to its south." The examples could be multiplied.

Countries that pursue an outward orientation opt for a market economy with institutions akin to those of the industrial countries. It is said that Marxist revolutions eat their children; there is a tendency among capitalist countries to abort their offspring.

The Dimming of Western Influence

Rapid growth in the Asian-Pacific region has caused a relative decline in the West's share of world production. The loss in influence this implies, however, is offset by the fact that, thanks to Pacific growth, the market countries as a group have increased their share in the world economy because the Asian-Pacific countries are operating successfully within an economic system oriented toward the West's, and similar to it. The demonstration effect need not erode the confidence of the West; rather, it should reinforce it. This is an important difference to bear in mind vis-à-vis the positions of the West and the communist East.

Yet there is no denying the unease that is felt in the West. The vitality of the Asian-Pacific countries, and the self-confidence radiating from Japan and the East Asian hub in particular, is affecting the standing of the West. Weaknesses have been exposed, especially in Europe, where a number of institutional changes and obstacles based on consideration of security and privilege rather than of audacity and experiment make for a less efficient economic system. The Asian-Pacific advances are widely regarded as a threat. We shall return to this problem in the concluding chapter.

For now, it suffices to notice how these new perceptions have dimmed Western influence. In the West, and particularly in Europe, there is a sense of grave economic and political difficulty.[75] The perception of Europe as a region in decline can also be detected in the Asian Pacific. Europe is viewed there as a continent undergoing "elegant stagnation"—a place to go for cultural education and sight-seeing. References to "Euro-gloom" and "old country disease" are frequent in Asian-Pacific newspapers and other writings.

Writing in *Foreign Affairs*, Fritz Stern describes the Japanese attitude as follows: "The Japanese have a nostalgia for European culture; they would like to reknit cultural ties that once were so close. But they are also exasperated by what they regard as Europe's decline into a museum of culture, into 'an old men's home,' whose inhabitants are content to live out their remaining days with whatever comfort they can find. They believe that the Europeans are morose, 'dying spiritually and economically,' unwilling to work, unwilling to compete or collaborate. Underneath the strictures remains the desire for good relations with Europe, for a better understanding with partners once considered inspiriting models."[76] Quoting this passage in his book on the trade problems of Japan and Europe, Masamichi Hanabusa, an official of the Japanese Ministry of Foreign Affairs, confirms that it aptly describes contemporary Japanese sentiments toward Western Europe.[77]

Again, *Japan in the Year 2000* talks of "the disease suffered by the industrialized countries."[78] As to the United States, Makoto Kikuchi, once a leading figure at MITI's electrotechnical laboratory, and one of the architects of Japan's electronics industry, identifies three phases in the emergence of that industry: "the age of learning," "the catch-up days," and "melancholia Americana."[79] Edward Feigenbaum notices a similar melancholia when he observes that "to live through what may be [the American Century's] waning years is a melancholy experience."[80]

Western stagnation and protectionism suggest that these and similar characterizations are not dramatic exaggerations. The Asian-Pacific message needs to be carefully considered in the established industrial countries. But whatever challenge the dynamism of the newcomers poses to the West, it does not imply that the basic economic system of the Western countries is in itself deficient; on the contrary, it signals the opportunities inherent in the system, as well as the drawbacks in failing to grasp those opportunities. The Asian-Pacific rise has taken place within an economic system that was perfected by the Western countries but has been gradually eroded there. The political challenge posed by Asian-Pacific growth to the Western industrial countries is totally different from that posed to the communist countries. The challenge for the West is to understand and grasp the new opportunities and to respond constructively.

THREE

A Wider Partnership

The theory of international trade has primarily to do with the advantages offered by liberal trade and by wider trade networks. Yet the public debate stresses the discomforts caused by new trading nations. What so often seems to be forgotten in this debate is that growth in one region can stimulate growth elsewhere. There are mutual advantages for all concerned. The scope for fruitful exchange increases; there are wider markets and better sources of goods and services; capital and investment opportunities (both domestic and foreign) are more plentiful; there are new technologies to use, new methods to emulate, more competition, and the stimulus of faster feedback.

These are the tenets of the often-neglected international trade theory and the generalizations that it invites. International contacts serve as a vehicle of productivity and inspiration. European growth reflects such impulses. E. A. Hall sums up European borrowing from the East as follows: "Perhaps European civilization could not have progressed so rapidly had it not possessed a remarkable faculty for assimilation—from Islam, from China, and from India. No other civilization seems to have been so widespread in its roots, so eclectic in its borrowings, so ready to embrace the exotic. Most have tended (like the Chinese) to be strongly xenophobic, and to have resisted confession of inferiority in any respect, technological or otherwise. Europe would yield nothing of the pre-eminence of its religion and but little of its philosophy, but in processes of manufacture and in natural science it readily adopted whatever seemed useful and expedient."[1] If today's established industrial countries can learn from what is happening in the Asian-Pacific region, it will not be the first time that the West has learned from the East. This chapter will describe past and present mechanisms of international trade and will suggest how growth in one region offers new opportunities to others.

The History

Throughout history there has been an interaction between the centers of Europe and the main cultures of Asia. It has varied in intensity, and there have been many shifts in the origin and principal direction of its main impulses. Moreover, the influences have passed both ways. Indeed, the "westernization of Asia" was preceded by the still more significant contributions made by Asia to Europe.[2] Present-day interdependencies are merely a continuation of this process.

At first, parallel civilizations developing in the East and West were close rivals in brilliance. Contact between the Mediterranean culture and the cultures of India and China took place through intermediaries; mutual perceptions were shadowy. Unrelated fragments of information were transmitted by tortuous routes and at great intervals. After the collapse of Rome, the European view of the East began to combine myth and reality. Fantasy held a strong grip even after Europe awoke from the dark ages. Whereas Marco Polo's reports were hardly believed, Mandeville's fables gained wide currency.

After the Roman collapse, Eastern cultures enjoyed an extended period of superiority. Until at least the time of Marco Polo, China was a "far greater civilization in both size and accomplishment than its contemporary, medieval Europe."[3]

The transfer of technology went from east to west. In China there was little interest in the "barbarians." The Chinese had an ethnocentric approach, considering themselves surrounded by inferior peoples. During the Ming Dynasty they did send out expeditions to explore the West; on reaching Africa, these expeditions reported having found little of interest besides giraffes.[4]

In contrast, Europe was outward-looking. Interest in the East and efforts to make contact emanated from Europe, and the "taste of the Orient"—the spices—added a strong material incentive to this spirit of curiosity. Beginning in the sixteenth century, the exploits of European explorers and adventurers ushered in a period of convergence between Asia and Europe. Now that direct contact was established, European travelers, traders, missionaries, and to some extent scholars increasingly began to replace Arab intermediaries as the vehicles of exchange, though within a framework and on terms established by their Asian hosts. For the Europeans in the East were there on sufferance. In China they were welcomed in the same way as tributaries. Japan quickly became closed to all but a few Dutch traders.

A telling problem for the Europeans was that they had little to sell that attracted the Chinese, for they "had few products of value to exchange for the spices and silks of more advanced economies."[5] Indeed, "the dominant fact for nearly three hundred years of . . . commercial intercourse, from the sixteenth to the nineteenth century, was that the Westerner desired the goods of the East and was able to offer little merchandise in return."[6] The problem of finding "something the Chinese wanted to buy" would prove to be particularly acute for the Americans.[7]

But these observations on the historical export difficulties of the West should be analyzed on the basis of the comparative cost theory and its proposition that even countries with a lesser all-around capacity must have something to sell.

If the Europeans and Americans really had nothing that the Chinese wanted to buy, trade would surely have ceased; terms of exchange would have become so unfavorable that the Chinese products would have become impossibly expensive. In fact, the Chinese imports were paid for in gold and, more important, in Mexican silver, for which there was a demand in China. Eventually the Europeans also set up a three-way trade; they brought spices not only back to Europe, but also to China in exchange for silk and tea. At a later stage, opium became part of the three-way trade of both Europe and the United States.[8]

The increase in trade with the East beginning in the sixteenth century was one of the reasons for an economic shift from the Mediterranean to Europe's Atlantic coast, especially since it took the form of direct sea-trade that cut out Arab intermediaries. By the late nineteenth century, the Western capacity for discovery had led not only to the exploration of new continents but also to new industrial and technological pursuits. At last, the West had the technology to produce goods for which there were markets in the East.

The Industrial Revolution brought Europe not only new tools and new exports, however, but new perceptions. Donald Lach offers the following summing up: "The Westerners of the industrial age, impressed by their own technical and organizational achievements, no longer felt awed by what they saw in the Orient. . . . European and American thinkers of the nineteenth century increasingly looked upon the countries of the East as centers of retardation, as a potential menace to the world which the Westerners seemed divinely destined to make over in their own image, and as an irritating reminder of the fact that decay and disintegration ultimately overtake even the most brilliant and powerful civilizations."[9] Thus the period of convergence ended in a century of Western dominance. Efforts at isolation were not tolerated. China and Japan were "opened."

The Japanese, less xenophobic than the Chinese, had once imported Chinese culture on a massive scale. Now they proved to be as skilled at learning from foreigners as ever the Europeans had been. They mastered the art of selective acculturation; they imported technologies and improved on them without losing their own culture and identity.

A similar strategy now characterizes the Asian-Pacific region as a whole, and it is this that has made possible the marked advances there. Rapid economic growth and technological progress in East Asia since World War II is again altering the relationships between Asia and the West. Complacent isolationism has been replaced by nervous integration, submission by competition, and war by economic rivalry. The economic signals coming from the East have gradually increased in intensity. The West is no longer the arbiter. As Hofheinz and Calder have put it, perhaps "the high noon of European and American industrial supremacy has passed, bringing to an end the brief period of a few hundred years in which Asia, especially the eastern part of Asia, did not dominate the world."[10]

Whether the Pacific Basin or the Atlantic Basin will have the more powerful effect on the future is an open question. It is entirely possible that the Pacific will come to dominate, and that the future will offer not so much a continuing "Westernization of Asia" as a more prominent role for Asia in the shaping of Europe and of the eastern United States.

The Asian-Pacific Market

Since the early 1960's there has been a rapid increase in imports into the Asian-Pacific market from all countries and country groups (see Table 8). Designed to meet the Asian-Pacific countries' increasing raw material requirements, this expansion has been made possible by their rapidly rising purchasing power and has been facilitated by the gradual implementation of freer trade policies. Imports from the United States increased nearly twentyfold between 1960 and 1983, and they are very important in an absolute sense. In relative terms, however—when measured as a percentage of the total import bill of the Asian-Pacific region—they actually declined somewhat (see Table 8). Imports from Europe (OECD) have also increased rapidly (if less so than those from the United States), but their relative importance on the Asian-Pacific market has declined considerably. The EEC share has declined even more (from 19.6 percent of Asian-Pacific imports in 1960 to 9.8 percent in 1983). This does not necessarily mean that the EEC is less well equipped to deal with a fast-growing market than the OECD. Rather, it reflects a diminishing of U.K. trade with Australia and New Zealand when the United Kingdom joined the EEC; this affected the EEC share more sharply than the share of the wider group of OECD countries. (It also of course partially accounts for the relatively poor European showing in the Asian-Pacific market.)

The reductions in the import shares of Europe and the United States (and also of Canada) have been paralleled by a dramatic increase in the shares gained by the Asian-Pacific countries themselves and by developing countries outside the region. In absolute terms, intraregional imports and imports from other developing countries have increased about twice as rapidly as imports from industrial countries. The main import from LDC's outside the Asian-Pacific group is oil. In Table 8, the spectacular increase in imports concentrated in the 1970's reflects the rise in oil prices. Between 1980 and 1983, the decline in oil prices led to a decline in LDC import share from 30 percent to 22 percent. Imports from other Asian-Pacific countries now represent by far the largest source of imports for the region; they have risen consistently in both absolute and relative terms.

Imports to Japan from the Asian-Pacific countries in rela-

TABLE 8

*Imports to the Asian-Pacific Region from Principal Countries
and Country Groups, 1960-1983*

Country	1960	1970	1980	1982	1983
	(U.S.$ billions)				
United States	2.9	9.4	51.9	54.8	55.5
Canada	0.4	1.3	6.8	6.7	6.5
Europe (OECD)	2.9	6.8	33.4	35.5	36.4
Non–Asian-Pacific					
LDCs (excl. China)	1.7	6.6	90.0	72.5	65.8
China	0.4	1.0	10.8	13.3	13.1
USSR, Eastern					
Europe, etc.[a]	0.1	0.9	3.0	2.6	2.3
Asian-Pacific					
countries	3.6	12.2	87.7	110.6	110.9
TOTAL	12.0	38.2	283.6	296.0	290.3
	(Percent of total Asian-Pacific imports)				
United States	22.5%	24.1%	17.5%	18.0%	18.6%
Canada	2.8	3.3	2.3	2.2	2.2
Europe (OECD)	22.1	17.6	11.3	11.7	12.2
Non–Asian-Pacific					
LDCs (excl. China)	12.9	17.1	30.4	23.8	22.0
China	2.8	2.6	3.6	4.3	4.4
USSR, Eastern					
Europe, etc.[a]	1.1	2.3	1.0	0.9	0.8
Asian-Pacific					
countries	28.4	31.6	29.6	36.3	37.1
TOTAL	92.6%	98.6%	95.7%	97.2%	97.3%

SOURCES: IMF 1963, 1975, 1984b. Data for Taiwan for 1980-82 from Republic of China 1984; for 1983, from Ministry of Economic Affairs and Euro-Asia Trade Organization, Taipei. Since IMF 1984b excludes Taiwan, exports to Taiwan from the various countries and country groups are taken from Taiwan's import figures.

NOTE: Totals do not sum to 100%, apparently because (a) a few exporting countries are not specified (but the figures are not significant), and (b) the country-specific figures suffer from errors and omissions.

[a]This category differs slightly in different years: for 1983 Cuba, Mongolia, and North Korea are included, and Rumania and Hungary are excluded.

tion to total Japanese imports rose from about 22 percent in 1960 to 27 percent in 1983. The rest of the region had much higher intraregional trade ratios; in 1983 the unweighted average—excluding Brunei and Papua New Guinea—was 44 percent. Australia, New Zealand, and Indonesia, which depend heavily on exports of primary commodities, with strong markets in Japan and the NICs, experienced the most rapid increases in this ratio. As to Korea and Taiwan, the oil price increases of the 1970's eliminated a previous increase in their regional import shares.

Imports from the Soviet Union and Eastern Europe have been insignificant, and between 1970 and 1983 these countries suffered the most pronounced decline in their share of the Asian-Pacific market. In the same period, China staged the most pronounced increase, but from a very small base.[11]

In assessing the importance of the Asian-Pacific market, it is instructive to consider how the exports to this market from the United States and other countries and country groups have developed as a share of their total exports. The Asian-Pacific market has expanded rapidly not only in an absolute sense but also, as indicated by Table 9, in relation to the exports of the United States, Canada, the non-Asian Pacific LDCs, and China. Export figures for Eastern Europe and Western Europe present a different picture. Exports to the Asian Pacific from the USSR and its satellites are few, and they show no definite pattern. It is nonetheless clear that, since the 1970's at least, they have failed to keep pace with Eastern bloc exports as a whole. This is not just a reflection of souring relations between the USSR and China (which resulted in a decline in Soviet exports to Hong Kong for reexport to China), since there has been a relative decline in exports to the other Asian-Pacific countries as well. (It should be noted that the figures in Table 9 exclude trade within the Eastern bloc, since any particular increase there might tend to obscure trading patterns elsewhere.) Western European exports to the Asian Pacific are considerable in value terms, but they have declined somewhat as a percentage of total exports. If intra-European trade is excluded (in order to minimize the effects of European integration on the trade pattern), we still find a slight downward shift in Europe's export share. This is largely accounted for by the marked decline in the share of U.K. exports to Australia and New Zealand.

TABLE 9

Exports to the Asian-Pacific Region as a Percentage of the Total Exports of Each Exporting Country or Country Group, 1960-1983

Country	1960	1970	1980	1982	1983
United States	13.1%	19.2%	21.2%	23.0%	24.7%
Canada	6.6	6.8	8.6	8.4	7.7
Europe (OECD)	5.8	4.6	3.7	4.3	4.5
Europe (OECD) (excl. intra-European trade)	13.4	13.6	11.4	11.8	13.1
Non–Asian-Pacific LDCs (excl. China)	6.5	12.5	15.8	16.9	15.8
China	19.5	54.1	54.2	52.7	52.7
USSR, Eastern Europe, etc. (excl. intra-trade)	3.3	9.9	5.1	4.7	4.1

SOURCES: Same as for Table 8.

It should be stressed that these figures for Asian-Pacific imports from the one or another country group do not give a complete picture of the new market opportunities. Thus the expansion of the Asian-Pacific market may have more significance for OECD Europe than is indicated by the direct export ratio from Europe to the Asian-Pacific region. Extensive importation of primary products into the Asian-Pacific countries creates new trading opportunities between Europe and the raw material-exporting countries. Because the Asian-Pacific region is far from self-sufficient in primary products, this triangular trade effect is very important.

New Sources of Supplies

The rationale for international trade is that it enables individual countries to acquire goods less expensively than if they had to produce everything themselves. It allows an international specialization that permits each country to concentrate on what it can produce best. Exports are a means of paying for imports. From a national point of view, exports are not an end in themselves—except to subscribers to mercantilist views that the final goal is to sit on a growing pile of gold and claims, acquired from foreigners. The advantages of international trade are so subtle that they elicit little comment from consumers. Much more likely to dominate the debate on trade are groups of producers who are hurt by import competition. This should not blind us, however, to the consumer advantages of having access to new and wider sources of supplies. By their response in the marketplace, consumers have demonstrated their considerable delight with the widened choices and lower prices made possible by Asian-Pacific suppliers. Producers squeezed by competition may protest that "there is nothing the East Asians can produce that we cannot produce as well"; that is evidently not the way consumers (and many buyers of semimanufactured and capital goods) have seen it.

Table 10 lists the principal countries and country groups importing from the Asian-Pacific region and presents the imports in dollar terms and as a percentage of each country's total imports. By both measures, all the countries listed in the table show a tremendous increase in imports from the Asian-Pacific region between 1960 and 1983. The greatest increases are in imports into the United States and China (although the Chinese base is small). The least impressive increase is registered for Western and Eastern Europe. The position of the Asian-Pacific region has nevertheless strengthened in all markets. Its highest shares are in the U.S. and Chinese markets, although its position on the Chinese market may be inflated by imports from Hong Kong that emanate from other countries. Its share of the Western European market is surprisingly small, and its share of the Eastern European market surprisingly large.

Asian-Pacific exports have proved very attractive and have made a very real contribution to the well-being of other peoples. This important contribution—which is the essence of

A Wider Partnership

TABLE 10

Principal Countries and Country Groups Importing
from the Asian-Pacific Region, 1960-1983

Country	1960	1970	1980	1982	1983
			(U.S.$ billions)		
United States	2.3	9.7	66.1	75.9	86.7
Canada	0.2	0.9	4.6	5.2	6.4
Europe (OECD)	3.3	6.8	52.3	47.5	48.6
Non–Asian-Pacific					
LDCs (excl. China)	1.9	4.6	42.6	50.9	41.5
China	0.1	0.8	7.6	7.2	8.7
USSR, Eastern					
Europe, etc.	0.4	0.9	7.6	7.6	6.3
			(Imports from Asia-Pacific as a percentage of total)		
United States	15.3%	22.8%	25.7%	29.8%	32.1%
Canada	3.7	6.7	7.5	9.1	10.1
Europe (OECD)	5.8	4.6	5.8	6.2	6.6
Non–Asian-Pacific					
LDCs (excl. China)	7.8	11.0	10.4	12.0	12.5
China	4.7	4.4	39.0	37.9	40.6
USSR, Eastern					
Europe, etc.	2.7	8.6	11.7	12.8	11.0

SOURCES: Same as for Table 8.

trade—should not be allowed to be obscured by those who
feel only the pressures of new competition and seek their own
immediate advantage. If the Asian-Pacific countries had not
been discriminated against by means of restrictive trade policies, consumers and buyers would have exercised their freedom of choice by opting for Asian-Pacific goods in still larger
quantities—and this in turn would have given exporters from
other regions a further expanding Asian-Pacific market for
their own goods.

Table 11 shows the share of Asian-Pacific exports that goes
to the various markets and how it changed between 1960 and
1983. A steadily decreasing proportion of Asian-Pacific exports goes to Europe (OECD). The increase in the purchasing
power of the oil countries in the 1970's meant an upward shift

TABLE 11

Exports from the Asian-Pacific Region to Principal Importing Countries and Country Groups as a Percentage of Total Asian-Pacific Exports, 1960-1983

Country	1960	1970	1980	1982	1983
United States	18.5%	26.8%	22.5%	23.5%	27.1%
Canada	1.8	2.6	1.6	1.7	2.0
Europe (OECD)	24.7	17.7	16.5	14.7	14.5
Non–Asian-Pacific LDCs (excl. China)	16.3	12.0	16.2	16.5	14.6
China	0.8	2.1	2.8	2.4	2.7
USSR, Eastern Europe, etc.	2.6	2.2	2.4	2.3	1.8
Asian-Pacific countries	26.5	32.5	36.2	36.3	34.5
TOTAL	91.2%	95.9%	98.2%	97.4%	97.2%

SOURCES: Same as for Table 8.

NOTE: Totals do not sum to 100%, apparently because (a) a few exporting countries are not specified (but the figures are not significant), and (b) the country-specific figures suffer from errors and omissions.

in this market's share of Asian-Pacific exports, and a reduction in even the U.S. share (which otherwise increased in the 23-year period). The share of exports going to other Asian-Pacific countries was very high, and on the increase.

International Movements of Factors of Production

The growth of new countries creates wider opportunities for international movements of factors of production. The Asian-Pacific countries are participating in this process. There has been a considerable movement of labor from Thailand, the Philippines, and Korea—often to oil-rich and labor-scarce countries in the Middle East and North Africa. Remittances of earnings from workers abroad are of some importance in the balance of payments of these countries.[12] Many of the workers go abroad to work on civil engineering projects for international contractors. Some of the most important international contractors are Japanese and Korean.

TABLE 12

Balance on Current Account for Asian-Pacific Countries, 1970-1982

(U.S.$ billions)

Country	1970	1979	1980	1981	1982
Japan	2.0	−8.7	−10.7	5.1	7.0
Korea	−0.6	−3.2	−5.3	−4.4	−2.7
Taiwan	0.0	1.3	0.0	1.4	3.3
Singapore	−0.6	−1.1	−1.6	−1.8	−1.3
Philippines	0.0	−1.3	−2.0	−2.3	−3.4
Indonesia	−0.3	1.7	2.9	−0.7	n.a.
Malaysia	0.0	1.6	−0.5	−2.9	−3.4
Thailand	−0.3	−1.9	−2.3	−2.6	−1.1
Papua New Guinea	—	−0.1	−0.3	−0.6	−0.5
Australia	−0.8	−1.9	−4.3	−8.5	−8.4
New Zealand	0.0	−0.5	−0.7	−1.2	−1.5
TOTAL	−0.6	−14.1	−24.8	−18.5	−12.0

SOURCES: World Bank 1984. For Taiwan, Republic of China 1984.
NOTE: Figures were not available for Hong Kong.

The Asian-Pacific countries are also involved in large-scale movements of capital. Japan exports an enormous amount of capital, thereby adding to the world supply of savings. Taiwan is also an exporter of capital. Australia and Korea lead in importing capital. Among the other developing Asian-Pacific countries, Malaysia and Thailand are moderate international borrowers. In order to finance high domestic investments, Singapore and Hong Kong have added to their substantial savings by engaging in private borrowing on the international markets.

A capital exporter puts real resources at the disposal of others in the form of a surplus on current account; capital importers have a deficit on current account. The current account for the Asian-Pacific countries for 1979-82 is shown in Table 12. The region as a whole has had net capital imports of U.S. $70 billion during this period and was more important as a market for goods and services than as a supplier.[13]

As shown in Table 13, Korea, the Philippines, Indonesia, and other LDCs of the region have run up a total external public debt of considerable magnitude. Only the Philippines, however, has not managed to service her debt. Korea has the highest ratio of foreign debt to GNP, but because of her outward orientation she has had no difficulties in servicing the debt.

The Asian-Pacific countries are also engaged in substantial two-way international direct investment activities. In the late 1960's Japan made a rapid effort to expand direct foreign investments in order to improve supplies of raw materials, as well as to ease other domestic growth constraints. For these

TABLE 13

*External Public Debt and Debt Service Ratios of Asian-Pacific LDCs,
1970 and 1982*

| | Total public and publicly guaranteed loans, disbursed | | | |
| | U.S.$ billions | | Pct. of GNP | |
Country	1970	1982	1970	1982
Korea	1.8	20.1	20.4%	28.3%
Hong Kong	<0.05	0.3	0.1	1.0
Singapore	0.2	1.4	7.9	10.0
Philippines	0.6	8.8	8.1	22.5
Indonesia	2.4	18.4	27.1	21.1
Malaysia	0.4	7.7	10.0	30.5
Thailand	0.3	6.2	4.9	17.4
Papua New Guinea	<0.05	0.7	5.8	32.8

| | Debt service as pct. of: [a] | | | |
| | GNP | | Exports | |
Country	1970	1982	1970	1982
Korea	3.0%	5.2%	19.4%	13.1%
Hong Kong	<0.05	0.2	<0.05	<0.05
Singapore	0.6	1.7	0.6	0.8
Philippines	1.4	2.6	7.2	12.8
Indonesia	0.9	2.6	6.9	8.3 [b]
Malaysia	1.7	2.9	3.6	5.1
Thailand	0.6	2.2	3.4	8.4
Papua New Guinea	0.1	4.1	—	10.2

SOURCE: World Bank 1984.

[a] Debt service is the sum of interest payments on and repayment of principal of external public and publicly guaranteed debt.

[b] This figure is for 1981.

purposes, she invested heavily in primary industries and manufacturing in the Asian-Pacific region. In the last few years, Japan has engaged in important direct foreign investments of a "tariff factory" type (that is, investments in manufacturing to circumvent barriers to Japanese exports) in both the United States and Europe.

Japanese investments for manufacturing purposes are sought after in many countries that are eager to benefit from the creation of new jobs and from the transfer of technology and management methods.[14] According to an official Japanese source: "Advanced Western countries are looking forward to the industrial cooperation of Japanese enterprises from the standpoints of revitalization of industry, mutual exchange of high technology in industry, and promotion of regional development. In developing countries, the expansion of Japanese enterprises is sought from the viewpoints of key industry development, export-oriented industrialization, regional development, and employment promotion."[15]

There is also a substantial and growing flow of direct investments from the United States and Europe to Japan and other Asian-Pacific countries. Table 14 shows the net direct private investment of the various Asian-Pacific countries between 1976 and 1982. Where a minus sign appears, the outflow of direct investments abroad exceeds the inflow of foreign investments at home. Comparative figures are given for the United States and the three major European direct investors. Japan is among the top four direct investors and in 1982 had larger net direct investments abroad than any other country.

Trade and factor movements resulting from Asian-Pacific growth will lead to new macroeconomic interrelationships. An increase in the number of countries participating in the world economy, and the concommitant lack of synchronization among individual business systems, would contribute to greater stability in the world economy taken as a whole. But

TABLE 14

Net Direct Private Investment of Asian-Pacific and Other Countries, 1976-1982

(U.S.$ billions)

Country	1976	1977	1978	1979
Japan	−1.9	−1.6	−2.4	−2.7
Korea	0.1	0.1	0.1	<0.05
Taiwan	0.1	<0.05	0.1	0.1
Singapore	0.7	0.3	0.7	0.9
Philippines	0.1	0.2	0.2	0.1
Indonesia	0.3	0.2	0.3	0.2
Malaysia	0.4	0.4	0.5	0.6
Thailand	0.1	0.1	0.1	0.1
Papua New Guinea	0.02	0.02	0.03	0.04
Australia	0.8	0.9	1.4	1.3
New Zealand	0.2	0.1	0.2	0.3
United States	−7.6	−8.2	−8.2	−13.4
United Kingdom	−2.4	−1.0	−2.7	−2.0
Germany	−1.4	−1.4	−2.1	−2.8
France	−0.6	0.9	0.9	0.5

Country	1980	1981	1982	1976-82
Japan	−2.1	−4.7	−4.1	−19.4
Korea	<0.05	0.1	−0.1	0.4
Taiwan	0.1	0.1	—	0.6
Singapore	1.7	1.8	2.1	8.2
Philippines	0.05	0.4	0.3	1.3
Indonesia	0.2	0.1	—	1.4
Malaysia	0.9	1.3	1.3	5.3
Thailand	0.2	0.3	0.2	1.0
Papua New Guinea	0.06	0.09	0.08	0.35
Australia	1.3	1.8	2.0	9.5
New Zealand	0.1	0.2	—	1.1
United States	−5.6	12.9	13.5	−16.7
United Kingdom	−2.1	−8.7	−2.6	−21.5
Germany	−3.1	−2.9	−2.5	−16.3
France	0.3	−2.2	−1.2	−1.4

SOURCES: World Bank 1983c. Data for 1982 are preliminary figures from World Bank 1984. Data for Taiwan from Kuo 1983: 208.

NOTE: A minus sign means that the outflow of direct investments exceeds the inflow. The 1976-82 sums for Taiwan, Indonesia, and New Zealand exclude 1982, for which data are not available.

that stability will also depend on whether the newcomers have more or less stable economies than the established countries. So far, both Japan and the Asian NICs have shown considerable stability and resilience, and therefore have probably had a steadying net effect on the international business situation.[16]

The Transfer of Technology

The Asian-Pacific countries have long been heavy importers of foreign technology. There are many modes of technology transfer: licensing, direct investment, training in connection with imports of technologically advanced equipment, research subcontracting, personnel exchanges, the use of foreign technical publications, attendance at international conferences, overseas studies, and industrial espionage.

The opportunity to import technology is a substantial advantage for newcomers. When an exchange of technology is part of an ordinary business transaction, it typically benefits both sides. Moreover, at least one of the Asian-Pacific countries—namely, Japan—has reached the stage where she is herself making major contributions to the stock of technology. The *Science Indicators*, published annually by the U.S. National Science Board, gives a number of statistics illustrating this advance. The Japanese Science and Technology Agency gives similar statistics in its *Indicators of Science and Technology* (Kagaku Gijutsu Yoran). R&D expenditures have increased more rapidly in Japan than in any of the other major countries. (Measured as a percentage of the GNP, they are lower than those of the United States and West Germany, but the statistic may be misleading because of the relatively low salary levels of young people in Japan; and if we look at just civilian R&D, it makes up a considerably larger proportion of the GNP than in the United States.) As a percentage of the labor force, the number of scientists and engineers engaged in R&D has expanded more rapidly in Japan than elsewhere. It is now higher than in West Germany, the United Kingdom, or France; in civilian R&D, it is probably higher than in the United States.[17]

The number of U.S. patents granted to Japanese inventors has risen rapidly. By 1982 it was higher than the total number of patents granted to West German, British, and Canadian inventors combined—though still only one-fourth the number of patents granted to Americans. In contrast, Japanese patents granted to U.S. inventors constituted only one-tenth of those granted to Japanese inventors.

Japan is still a major importer of technology, but she has now become an exporter of technology as well. Royalties paid still exceed royalties earned, but this is more a reflection of Japan's past than of her present. Data on payments for newly concluded contracts show that Japan has had a surplus every year since 1972, and that these surpluses have increased considerably. In 1980, receipts on new contracts were apparently almost three times as high as payments on new contracts.[18] Although the statistical material is sometimes incomplete, it leads to the unmistakable conclusion that Japan has been a current net exporter of technology for many years.

That Japan is no longer just an importer and imitator of technology, but an inventor and an exporter, means more rapid technological progress. It means that great new resources are available for exploring new technologies. Perhaps even more important, the competitive pressures of a new techno-rivalry will stimulate the United States and Europe to greater efforts than ever before. Assessments by leading research institutions suggest that technological progress is now in a phase of acceleration.[19] The double contribution of the Japanese is surely an important factor in this phenomenon.

New Competition

In order for the market system to work, there must be competition. An important contribution of the Asian-Pacific newcomers is the new competitive pressures they bring to bear. The complaints by those who fail to withstand the pressures should not be allowed to obscure the importance of this contribution to the strength of the economic system. Such complaints should rather be taken as a signal that the Asian-Pacific countries are playing an important role.

Competition makes resource utilization more efficient; it forces firms to eliminate slack if they wish to keep their customers. It also promotes growth by stimulating the search for improvements. An intensification of trade will speed up these processes. Trade prompts a more determined search for superior solutions, for with more competitors around, there is a greater risk of being left behind. Trade facilitates the search process by making information more readily available. Longer production runs make it easier to recoup fixed search costs. Competition from more countries will result in increased pressures on governments to provide good economic conditions, to remain competitive, and to attract factors of production and prevent them from leaving for greener pastures.

FOUR

The Asian-Pacific Threat

Some observers belittle Asian-Pacific achievements. Others view Asian-Pacific growth as a threat to the international community. In an effort to reconcile the two contradictory viewpoints, it is sometimes argued that this menacing growth was achieved by methods that exploited domestic labor and discriminated against other countries. The "threat" doctrine now plays a large role in emotional political arguments, in discussions on economic policy affairs, and in newspaper writings. Governments, industrial organizations, and trade unions devote an increasingly large amount of time and energy to the trade problems with Japan, the Asian NICs, and the other emerging Asian-Pacific countries. Politicians try to explain why they have failed to deliver; business leaders try to excuse their inability to compete; trade unionists resent the ready exposure of their lack of realism by outside competition.[1]

There have been a succession of missions to Tokyo to pressure Japan to "open up." In an article on foreign missions to Tokyo, the *Far Eastern Economic Review* of June 11-17, 1982, nominated as its favorite protester a certain Portuguese official who asked that the Japanese accept more imports of port wine and dried fish; he was echoing an identical request made by a previous Portuguese representative in the blessed year of 1542.

The threat doctrine is also promulgated in academic treatises by political scientists. Roy Hofheinz, former Director of the East Asian Research Center at Harvard, and Kent Calder, former Executive Director of Harvard's Program on United States-Japan Relations, see many dangers in Asian-Pacific growth. They assert that U.S. economic prosperity depends on keeping abreast of East Asia. Otherwise, they predict, the dollar will shrink, the energy import bill will rise, inflation will advance, the industrial heartland will decline, investments will be more difficult, expanding markets will be lost, and America will become a less attractive investment target than East Asia. There will be a vicious cycle of intensified dissatisfaction, higher welfare burdens, a more skewed income distribution, deepening social ills, and a major redistribution of power within the United States.[2] A growing academic literature also deals with the political and economic implications of the Asian-Pacific challenge, and the region's supposed "collision course" with the West.[3]

The Four Problems

The friction, and in particular the trade friction, generated by these anxieties threatens the international economic framework, and it is important to understand the extent Asian-Pacific growth actually does constitute a menace to other trading nations. There are many imaginary and some real problems.

First, when newcomers carve out for themselves an increasing share of the world economy, the relative share of other countries is inevitably reduced. Established countries that fail to develop rapidly will suffer a relative decline. This has happened before, and it is to be hoped that it will happen again. On account of the successes of other countries, the U.S. share of world GDP declined from more than 50 percent to 25 percent between 1950 and 1982. In the nineteenth century, the relative decline of Britain was another striking example of this process, and surely not a regrettable one. "Indeed," says

Nathan Rosenberg, "it was an extraordinary aberration that this small island in the North Sea should *ever* have accounted for one-half of the world's total output of coal, over one-half of its pig iron (as it did in 1870), and more than three quarters of the iron and steel products in international markets."[4]

Nevertheless, the established countries may well perceive the weakening of their dominance as a political threat. If the pleasure and pride of leaders lie in being unrivaled, a relative decline in the political and economic position of their nations can only be resented. Thus the advantages of being involved in larger partnerships may be overlooked or insufficiently appreciated—or may simply seem to be outweighed by the disadvantages. Countries with different economic and social systems from those of the successors are the most likely to be inconvenienced.

Second—and this is an extension of the relative decline argument—established countries may be apprehensive that growth elsewhere will entail a deterioration of their national security. Although an elaboration on these considerations is beyond the scope of this essay, one particular aspect of the problem should be mentioned. Japan—a source of sensitive high-tech information—is arguably a relatively easy target for industrial espionage by the Soviet Union. For that reason, if for no other, U.S. government officials feel that the United States cannot afford to have its preeminence in high technology eroded by Japan. Their rationale is that a U.S. technological edge is needed to offset Soviet superiority in firepower.[5]

These considerations have prompted a certain amount of technological protectionism in the United States.[6] But because most high-tech developments in electronics, bioengineering, and new materials are "dual purpose" technologies, civilian and military applications are difficult to separate. Furthermore, it has been argued that security-inspired protectionism which goes beyond protecting products usually thought of as classified and restricted for military purposes may assist U.S.

economic competitiveness and alleviate a third problem—the adjustment problem.

The adjustment problem is the crux of the matter. Although real, it is often misunderstood or exaggerated—sometimes to the point where it sounds as if competition from low-cost Asian NICs and high-tech Japan threatens the established economies with far-reaching deindustrialization or annihilation. But the Asian-Pacific countries could not produce everything for everyone even if they wanted to. And it is unlikely that they would want to, for this would imply a desire to sit on a growing mountain of financial claims on other countries. As the theory of comparative costs tells us, it is relative, not absolute, productivities that give the best trading opportunities.

That some sectors will be outcompeted is of course undeniable. After all, the very idea of trade and specialization implies that some things should be let go in order to make room for other and better things. The refusal to see this, and to accept it, is part of the common—and exaggerated—fear of adjustment. This is not to say that the transition can be frictionless. There will indeed be adjustment difficulties. Factors of production are not completely mobile: investments in factories, machinery, and human capital cannot be shifted freely from one occupation or region to another. And there are costs associated with these immobilities. In a detached analysis, however, these costs should be looked upon as investments; the costs of rearranging the economy are investments in a more productive economy.

Since those who will bear the investment costs will not necessarily recover them directly, they are likely to protest, and their protests may well result in far more than occasional protectionism. The inevitable inflexibilities may be greatly increased by legislation and contract. The lower the mobility, the more difficult it will be to respond to the impulses of change. The greater the inflexibilities, the more numerous and vociferous the protests of those hurt by the new competition. Structural problems accumulate, and a vicious cycle of non-change ensues. The greater the inertia, the higher the investment costs in shifting resources from one occupation to another. It is quite possible to burden an economy with so many occupational and geographical restrictions on factor movements that it appears more advantageous to subsidize and protect production than to submit to the alternative, which is then non-production. Such thinking has influenced much of government policymaking in Europe.

Within an economy, a low capacity for adjustment is likely to be accompanied by a reduction in the capacity for innovation. In isolation, on a purely domestic level, the effects need not be serious. But within an international context—which cannot be ignored—they become momentous: when the fat of rents from technological leads has been consumed, and the reserves have been used up, and factor mobility (and the downward mobility of factor prices) is low, unabated outside competition may result in an underutilization of factors of production damaging enough to precipitate a serious decline in national income. An economy that produces such situations is not viable. A country cannot simply withdraw from the international market to protect itself from competition. The avoidance of adjustment problems by withdrawal can lead not only to a drop in income but to still more serious adjustment problems. Isolationism produces low real income levels because it foregoes the gains from trade. Open economies with high adjustment capacities have high and growing real income levels. But open economies that grow arthritic in their capacity to adjust find their high income levels eroded. Protectionism causes these levels to erode faster, and is a process that soon creates greater adjustment problems than those it is designed to meet.

Foreign competition does not cause these difficulties; it only exposes them. A protectionist elimination of foreign competition does not cure the difficulties; it compounds them. But this truth is often disputed. There are many different interpretations of the sources of the problems, and as many proposed remedies. These interpretations can, and do, cause major controversies in international and domestic politics. Antagonisms arise when the foreign competition is perceived as discriminatory, allegedly preventing imports and subsidizing exports. This is interpreted as an unfair practice and as a complication in adjusting to foreign competition.

Such antagonisms make up a fourth—and very real—problem. It consists of the negative effect of trade friction on international relations, and it feeds on a need for scapegoats. For various reasons—one of them a highly successful triangular trade in raw material imports and manufactured exports—Japan and the Asian NICs have become particularly vulnerable to scapegoatism.[7]

Asian-Pacific Competition as a Source of Adjustment Difficulties

Before Japan achieved real wage levels higher than the EEC average, and before she came to be perceived as a threat in the field of high technology, what the established industrial countries feared most from Japan was low-wage competition. They accordingly applied discriminatory trade policies against her until well into the 1960's.[8] The shift from low-productivity excuses for these policies to high-productivity excuses took place in an embarrassingly short period. As a diplomatic circus act, it was impressive: an energetic leap from protestations against an inundation of the market with low-quality products to protestations against a flooding of the market with superior-quality products.

To disregard comparative costs and argue that it is impossible to compete with a low-wage, low-productivity country is as erroneous as it is to argue that it is impossible to compete with a high-wage and technologically advanced country. Since no country can produce everything for everyone, each country will experience comparative advantages and disadvantages. Thus, in a book published in the mid-1930's on the effects of East Asian industrialization and competition, G. E. Hubbard noted—as we may find some pleasure in observing—that the competitive edge of Japan was blunted because "the turnover of labor [was] uneconomically high."[9] It should also be remembered that the Asian-Pacific region has for long periods had negative current account balances.

Robert Z. Lawrence has shown that, contrary to prevailing views, there was no deindustrialization in the United States between 1973 and 1980. From 1980 to 1982 the manufacturing sector had difficulties, but no more so than could have been predicted from earlier experiences of the effects of a domestic depression and a high dollar exchange rate on manufacturing employment and trade balances.[10] Although European countries have undergone some deindustrialization, their trade with the Asian-Pacific region cannot be the cause of it, since no country has had more trade with that region than the United States.

Adjustment pressures from Asian-Pacific competition have come at a time when developments in the established industrial countries have reduced their responsiveness to change. As a consequence, much attention has been directed toward the supposed effect of the competition on employment levels. But such increases in unemployment as have occurred should be attributed not so much to the pressure for change as to the conditions that have reduced responsiveness to change, for it is not possible to eliminate Asian-Pacific competition without serious costs to the economies of old and new industrial countries alike. In the absence of this competition, the potential gains from a wider partnership and a strong demonstration effect would be replaced by the inevitable losses resulting from isolation and conflict.

Like a successful new technology, trade is an instrument that makes it possible to acquire a greater quantity of goods and services for a given input of labor. In the past, waves of new technological progress have created unemployment scares, and new openings in international trade have been having the same effect. Equally persistent, these scares are also equally ill-founded. The short-run transition difficulties are real, but if we do not accept the investment costs and sacrifices necessary to reach a more productive level, there will be more old-style jobs but less new income. Like technological progress, trade makes it possible to create new employment to meet the new demand created by a more efficient use of resources. The mechanization of agriculture resulted in an enormous loss of employment in old agricultural jobs. The mechanization of industry also resulted in fewer jobs—and fewer drudgeries. Similarly, the expansion of international trade resulted in many jobs lost thanks to imports. Had all this not happened, however, we would all be working harder and longer—not because there would be more employment opportunities, but because it would be necessary for subsistence.

Yet it is misleading to speak of jobs "lost" as a result of trade, just as it would be misleading to speak of jobs "lost" thanks to the introduction of the wheel. Jobs are lost because of recessions, depressions, inflexibilities, and labor market conflicts. Trade and technological progress precipitate a shift from old to new jobs and provide greater freedom of choice as a result of a more efficient use of resources and higher incomes. Moreover, those who express concern about the employment effects of the new imports are evidently unaware of the new employment available in the expanding export sector, analogous to the new employment connected with new technology.

The new concerns about employment have spawned a rapidly expanding literature that attempts to measure the "losses." Since 1979 a continuing OECD study has reviewed this literature.[11] The OECD study finds imports from the NICs only became cause for concern "in the wake of the 1974-75 recession, when slow growth, high unemployment, and balance-of-payments difficulties combined to inhibit the process of industrial adjustment."[12] This tells us something about the true nature of the trade scare.

Using a variety of measures of direct and indirect employment effects of imports from the new countries, all the studies surveyed by the OECD conclude that the employment "losses" have been much less serious than the threat literature has made them out to be: "Despite [their] diversity it is reassuring to note that all the studies converge in concluding that the impact of actual or projected changes in trade flows [on employment] is small for the countries concerned."[13] Imports, although rapidly rising, have been matched by rising exports. The Asian-Pacific imports are a small percentage of total imports and an even smaller percentage of total production and consumption. Finally, the employment really lost as a result of depression and inflation and—in some sectors—distortive wage increases above the average has been much greater. Moreover, the employment "lost" because of technological progress and—in some sectors—because of demand changes resulting from shifts in tastes and from low income elasticities has also outweighed the employment "lost" because of the expansion of trade with the NICs.

As the OECD study concludes, "excessive concern in advanced industrial countries about competition from the developing countries in general and NICs in particular often reflects a failure to recognize the strength of the basic economic forces at work to ensure mutually beneficial relationships between trading partners."[14] What has impaired "the basic economic forces" referred to here is the old industrial countries' inflexibilities and their low capacity to adjust. Exactly the same problems impede the trade with Japan.

Asian-Pacific Protectionism as a Source of Adjustment Difficulties

The industrial policies and trade policies of Japan and the Asian NICs have been much criticized by those affected by the new competition. Those policies have been blamed for adding to whatever adjustment difficulties the established countries have encountered. There are two different kinds of accusations. One is that Japan and the NICs do not let in imports. The other is that they encourage exports by industrial policy "targeting" and subsidies. The two accusations are somewhat contradictory, since import protectionism draws factors of production away from export sectors. But they nevertheless coexist.

Among the Asian NICs, Taiwan had the largest export surplus to the United States for 1977-82. Yet Taiwan has relatively few industrial policy interventions and a fairly open trade regime. Hong Kong had the second largest export surplus to the United States, but it had no import obstacles and no industrial policies in operation. Singapore, which has low import barriers but a number of industrial policies, experienced substantial import surpluses from the United States. Korea, which presents a more complex trade picture vis-à-vis the United States, is frequently in the red despite various import barriers and an ambitious industrial policy. If we look at current accounts rather than trade balances, the United States shows a stronger overall position than the Asian NICs. This mixed picture of industrial policies and trade outcomes suggests (as does trade theory) that the difficulties in adjusting to competition from the Asian NICs must have some explanation other than the trade and industrial policies of these countries.

Undeniably, some of the Asian NICs that place considerable adjustment pressures on the established countries do impose a variety of trade obstacles. Although these obstacles reduce the productivity of the countries imposing them more than they restrict the net exports of the countries encountering them, they are nevertheless the subject of much criticism (and do create problems for certain export industries). Some of the protectionist measures taken by Western industrial countries are retaliatory. For the sake of their own efficiency and for diplomatic reasons, the NICs would do well to reduce these barriers and to assume GATT obligations as well as GATT rights. Their failure to do so, however, explains only part (and perhaps only a small part) of the present discrimination against them—after all, free-trading Hong Kong is also being discriminated against.[15]

Turning to Japan, we find that since the early 1960's she has gradually liberalized her trade policies.[16] Japanese tariff levels are lower than those of almost all other countries. Japan has a number of quantitative restrictions (QRs) on agricultural imports and a handful of other items.[17] These restrictions, however, are smaller than those of most European countries; if we include covert QRs (the so-called "orderly marketing agreements," or OMAs) and "voluntary export restraints" (VERs), which are numerous in Europe and the United States, the quantitative restrictions of Europe and the United States exceed those of Japan by a wide margin.[18] Furthermore, whereas Japanese QRs have been reduced, U.S. and European QRs have increased significantly since the mid-1970's. Many of the U.S. and European restrictions are specifically intended to limit imports from Japan and the Asian NICs, whereas the restrictions of these countries are applied on a nondiscriminatory basis. A confidential study by the OECD in November 1984 entitled "Costs and Benefits of Protection," which drew on published and unpublished material, gives support to the view that U.S. and EEC tariff and nontariff protection had increased since 1980, when it already exceeded that of Japan.

Considering this factual background, it would perhaps be more reasonable to criticize Japan for operating a network of elusive but effective nontariff trade barriers (NTBs). Undoubtedly, the Japanese do use many such trade barriers—as do other countries, perhaps with even greater frequency. Under pressure from the United States and the EEC, Japan has eliminated many of these barriers, as required by, for instance, the Tokyo Round GATT agreements. Many other countries have instead moved in the opposite direction. It has often proved difficult to pinpoint Japanese restrictive practices, although many feel affected by them. It should be remembered, however, that many of the difficulties and frustrations experienced by U.S. and European would-be exporters are attributable to difficulties created by the Japanese cultural mentality and way of doing things rather than to obstacles created by official decisions. The many-layered distribution system, which complicates marketing efforts, and the fact that the Japanese prefer not to work for foreigners are examples of such complications.

A variety of alleged hindrances—and their potential for causing ill will among potential exporters to Japan, and among the Japanese for being accused of being Japanese—have been entertainingly reviewed by Endymion Wilkinson in *Misunderstanding, Europe Versus Japan.*[19] A less amusing but more official statement of the same conclusions is offered by a committee of "wise men"—some American, some Japanese—appointed by the President of the United States and the Prime Minister of Japan to report on the economic relations between the two countries. Chapter 5 of this report addresses the question "Japan's Market: Open or Closed?" It finds Japan's market to be more open than most, but complicated—for outsiders—by virtue of being Japanese.[20]

The large bilateral deficits experienced by the United States

and the EEC countries in their trade with Japan are sometimes cited as a simplistic "proof" of Japanese protectionism.
A lack of domestic raw material resources means that Japan
necessarily has an export surplus of manufactures and an import surplus of primary commodities, and this is likely to be
reflected in wide bilateral deficits and surpluses. By importing
primary commodities, Japan creates markets for still other
countries. It is an overall, rather than a bilateral, balance that
is needed. The Japanese export surplus to the large EEC market is not much greater than the EEC export surplus to
Switzerland. The U.S. deficit in the trade with Japan is usually—that is, when the U.S. current account is in balance—not
much greater than the U.S. deficit in trade with Western Europe. As Gary Saxonhouse has shown in econometric work
on cross-country trade patterns, factors other than protectionism (distance, for example) account for a relatively low
amount of manufactured imports into Japan.[21]

We cannot rule out the possibility that there is some basis
for the accusations that Japanese trade policy is surrepti-
tiously protectionist, particularly when they emanate not only
from the established countries but from Japan's neighbors.[22]
But whatever the truth of the accusations, it must be understood that the removal of Japanese trade obstacles would
make Japan, not less competitive, but more so. Partly because
of Western pressure, Japan has been liberalizing her import
system for many years. This has not impaired Japan's trade
performance; rather, it has added to her export capacity, free-
ing resources from inefficient import-competition activities
and making them available for the export industries.

A further liberalization of Japanese export policies would
help potential exporters to Japan by facilitating entry and by
formulating clearer rules of the game. These are needed to
warrant the high initial marketing costs for a big market,
which are very different from what American and European
companies are used to. But further Japanese liberalization

measures would also help Japanese exporters. Protectionism, whether in Japan or elsewhere, does not reduce imports and expand exports. On balance, it reduces both imports and exports. Similarly, as has been vividly demonstrated by Japan, a liberalization of import policies increases both imports and exports.

Reviewing U.S.-Japanese trade problems, the 1984 annual report of the U.S. Council of Economic Advisers concluded that "the point is that Japanese protectionism, like all protectionism, distorts the pattern of trade in such a way as to hurt both countries on net; but it is not a major source of the Japanese trade surplus."[23] These conclusions are reached over and over again by those whose business it is to make careful evaluations. Yet the accusatory viewpoint is maintained tenaciously. In one of its variants, the yen is held to be undervalued in order to facilitate a flood of exports. In addressing the issue, the Council of Economic Advisers concludes that "no aspect of this view stands up well to the facts. . . . Although the Japanese authorities practice occasional exchange market intervention, their intervention has, if anything, prevented a further decline of the yen relative to the dollar."[24]

Japan is criticized not only for extravagant protectionism but also for sophisticated and unfair promotional policies to conquer the industrial future. Some typical accusations are (1) that major exports and exporters are "targeted" (a militaristic term for the less fancy concept of industrial policymaking); (2) that the government sponsors cooperation among firms in research and development; (3) that there is much less access to research institutions in Japan than there is in Europe, and still less than in the United States; (4) that the Japanese patent system makes it hard for foreigners to protect their rights in Japan; and (5) that next-generation industries are given protection and subsidy—for instance, by government procurement contracts during the development phase.

A number of counter-arguments can be offered. In considering the possible explanations and the lessons of Asian-Pacific growth earlier, we found that the importance often attributed to industrial policy has never been well demonstrated. The point should be reaffirmed here, and it should be emphasized that the industrial policies of Japan and the Asian NICs do not create great adjustment problems for the Western industrial countries. In its extensive review of foreign industrial "targeting" and its effects on U.S. industries, the U.S. International Trade Commission concludes that "evidence to support the claim that industrial targeting benefits the targeting country has been inconclusive." "Such evidence," the report continues, "generally consists of a selection of successful industries in successful countries, assertions that their success is due to targeting, and conclusions that the country's success is due to the targeting of these industries." The report further points out that "although it is known that targeting can change the mix of industries within a country, no one has clearly demonstrated that targeting adds to the general economic welfare of a country."[25]

These are general observations—and there is much material to draw from. Many countries that are critical of Japanese "targeting" spend much money and effort on industrial policy—often more than Japan. On the specifics of Japanese targeting, the ITC report concludes that "targeting seems to have had only a small role in some of these successes [of Japanese export industries]. . . . Some targeted industries have remained weak competitors. The role of targeting in the Japanese economy has declined as the Japanese government has reduced its interference with the market."[26] The 1984 report of the Council of Economic Advisers to the President finds that "industrial policy has a mixed record in Japan and has been unsuccessful in Europe" and that "the net effect of [Japan's industrial] policies on economic growth is not clear."[27]

The extent of Japanese industrial policy is frequently exaggerated out of all proportion. Government funding of R&D

performed in the business enterprise sector is low. In 1979 it was 1.4 percent, compared with 30 percent for the United States and the United Kingdom and 20 percent for France and West Germany.[28] As to the government share of total R&D expenditures, it is rising in Japan but is lower than in the United States and the major Western European countries.

Generally there are few government subsidies to Japanese manufacturing. Only one industry receives subsidies amounting to more than 0.1 percent of the GNP originating in that sector. (This sector is not electronics, but food processing.) According to Saxonhouse, "examination of the familiar instruments of industrial policy indicates that Japan gives less formal aid and comforts to her high-technology sectors than do the governments of most other advanced industrialized economies. Targeting is largely reserved for agriculture."[29]

There seems to be a widespread feeling in the United States that the Japanese have freeloaded off American R&D spending. The easy access to U.S. universities and research institutions has no parallel in Japan, where almost all scientific research is carried out within the big firms or in ventures initiated by MITI and other organizations. Furthermore, the mobility of researchers among companies in the United States creates a leakage that Japanese firms can probably benefit from. In contrast, there is no such traffic in Japan. An additional obstacle to gaining access to Japanese research activities is of course the language barrier.

To reduce freeloading, there has been an increase in U.S. technological protectionism that is not wholly inspired by security considerations. Results of industrial research funded by the U.S. Government are not freely available. Moreover, "unless a specific government waiver is obtained, the right to sell or use any government patent in the United States may be limited only to firms manufacturing substantially in the United States."[30] Interestingly enough, the Japanese have simultaneously made moves to open up government-funded and government-sponsored research results. "At the same time as American technology policy is becoming markedly more protectionist, Japanese technology policies are beginning to approximate some important elements of the American policies of the 1970's."[31]

The "White Peril"

The economic growth of Japan and the Asian NICs has created strong adjustment pressures for the established industrial countries. But the major problem is not the pressures themselves. Rather, it is the difficulties the industrial countries have in responding to them. Higher standards of living have permitted greater flexibility in life outside work, but they also seem to have introduced greater inflexibility into work life. Restrictive practices, whether negotiated by labor market organizations or legislated by governments, are intended to do away with some perceived hardships and to shield workers from change. Extensive welfare arrangements—and the taxes to finance them—have the same laudable motives, and so do the increasing number of regulations and rules that cater to the drive for "economic security." In the process, however, an increasing number of domestic trade obstacles are built up, creating distortions on the micro level that both are harmful in themselves and make macroadjustments more difficult. Prosperity is frittered away on attempts to preserve the status quo and placate distributional alliances. In short, these practices contain the seeds of their own destruction.[32]

The immediate post-war period saw a considerable dismantling of barriers to both domestic and foreign trade. Later, there was a continued reduction of foreign trade barriers but a parallel build-up of obstructions to domestic trade. Since the mid-1970's certain foreign trade barriers have continued to be dismantled, but on balance (and especially in the Western industrial countries), new foreign trade barriers are being erected while simultaneously (and despite efforts at deregulation) domestic trade obstacles continue to multiply.

The problems resulting from increased domestic and foreign trade barriers can be responded to in three possible ways: (1) there can be an intensification of efforts to dispel the pressures for adjustment by raising the foreign trade barriers; (2) there can be stronger measures to intensify domestic trade barriers in an effort to compensate those affected by adjustment pressures and shield them from the hardships of change; and (3) there can be measures to increase the adjustment capacity, measures that would entail dismantling both domestic and foreign trade barriers.

The first two methods have many short-run political attractions since they can be made to seem to offer a passage without privation. They can be blended into regulations and restrictions, work-sharing and prepensioning, and subsidies and protectionism. In other words, the welfare state can be extended into industrial policy. They are so attractive that it has proved hard to prevent manpower programs and other positive adjustment schemes that purportedly promote flexibility from being hijacked to serve the needs of the past rather than those of the future. Yet these two methods do not only invite hardships in the long run. The concern for economic security can threaten economic security. Stagnation brings its own changes.

Like charity, free trade begins at home. It is difficult to combine extensive domestic trade barriers with a lack of foreign trade barriers. It is also impossible to preserve high standards of living by withdrawing from competition and change. There is no such option, because these very standards have been achieved by extensive division of labor and successful participation in world markets. A rejection of this successful process would entail painful adjustments: away from export industries and down from present income levels. International trade is a machine—an invention that, like the creations of technological progress, constitutes a basis for welfare. Current protectionism is the politics of Mr. Ludd.

The most serious threat to the world economy is Western protectionism: first, a gradual increase in domestic trade barriers that are harmful in themselves; then, to add to the damage, an erection of foreign trade barriers; and then, in response to the mounting problems that result, not change but measures that only reinforce domestic and foreign trade barriers alike. The effect of these actions is to intensify friction between friends and former friends. This "White Peril" is a danger not only to the embattled industrial countries themselves but also to their trading partners. It threatens the future of both present trading partners and potential ones, developing countries that would otherwise be interested in advancing themselves by the methods that once made the old industrial countries—and now make the Asian NICs—so successful. The Western search for Asian scapegoats only magnifies the danger. Real problems are obscured; real possibilities are ignored. A new competitor can be a new customer—for those who have something to offer. But a preoccupation with "security first" and a vituperative attitude toward newcomers have sapped the West's vitality.

The Euro-Problem

Although there have been general tendencies toward obstructionism in all the established industrial countries, the capacity to adjust has declined most seriously in Europe. "Europe often looks for safety first—wars, recession, and old age have made it that way," says the *Economist* in an article describing "how Europe has failed." It adds that "this natural caution may prove suicidal now that the world is in the midst of a deep technological and economic change. America and Japan have been racing to meet this challenge—and seem to be prospering."[33] Impressive post-war growth facilitated over-commitments to new welfare programs and so forth. Gradually, such commitments took their toll on the economy and proved increasingly unrealistic, and now—when outside conditions require greater mobility and creativity and forward-looking entrepreneurship—they become almost impossible to honor. The decline in performance has exacerbated the struggle for income shares and has endangered privileges. Both entrepreneurial expectations and resources have become depressed.

The OECD's *Economic Outlook* has noted that "most European countries have made less complete supply-side adjustment to changes in factor prices and the structure of demand than has Japan, and may generally have been less innovative and dynamic in the newly developing sectors than have Japan and the United States."[34] These difficulties are also reflected in the relatively low capacity of many European countries to generate new jobs. Between 1960 and 1983, civilian employment increased by an average of 1.9 percent a year in the OECD; in Japan it increased by 1.1 percent, and in the EEC by just 0.3 percent.

In his study *Can America Compete*, Robert Lawrence compares the U.S. and European performances. Unlike the United States, Europe has been deindustrializing since the early 1970's. The statistical material on employment, production, profit rates, and investment points to "the marked contrast in European economic performance before and after 1973, a contrast that is particularly evident in data on European industrial performance."[35] As Lawrence points out, the European governments have assumed greater responsibilities than the U.S. or Japanese governments for providing job security and steady increases in the standard of living. These guarantees were costless before their effects made themselves felt, but became particularly costly after the shocks of the 1970's, which required flexibility and mobility.[36]

In its *Annual Economic Report* for 1982-83, the Commission of the European Communities made the following observation: "It is in particular apparent that the Japanese and United States examples have in common a positive employment creation record, a more positive record of enterprise profitability, of labor cost adaptability to economic circumstances, and—for reasons linked to social structure—of less onerous labor regulations that place constraints on the use of production capacity."[37] In its 1983-84 *Report*, the Commission has this to say: "With cyclical trends gradually turning in more favourable directions, there remains the important question of whether the European economy is now on a course of more fundamental structural improvement. . . . The assessment must at best be cautious. . . . As regards the major industrial technologies, the evidence continues to show a lagging performance in Europe."[38] And in the 1984-85 *Report*: "The Community is now having to respond to the challenge of an emerging inferiority, by comparison with the United States and Japan, in industrial capacity in new and fast-growing technologies. . . . The deteriorating world trade performance of the Community in such fields as computers, micro-electronics, and equipment is now generally recognized."[39]

The ills of Europe, and the Eurogloom they have caused, are also treated in two collections of essays edited by Andrea Boltho and Ralf Dahrendorf and a study by Michael Emerson, all three authors with an EEC background.[40] As Jean Waelbroeck notes in a review article on these books, there was a "silly season" in European policymaking characterized by exaggerated beliefs about what could be legislated rather than produced and what could be fine-tuned in the face of enacted rigidities. There was a "degeneration of democracy, as secondary political systems, based on negotiations and conflicts between interest groups, acquired power and legitimacy."[41]

Some Atlantic Strains

The adjustment difficulties in Europe and the trade imbalances of a rising dollar in the United States have provoked interventions to limit the pressures of competition from the outside and soften the impact at home. Aware of the dangers of traditional protectionism, the Europeans have tried out subventionist industrial policies in the hope that these can also bring about some structural changes. But the Atlantic and European experiences have indicated that when relative prices are determined by subsidy rather than by production costs and efficiencies, there will be painful conflicts. A still more negative example of these mechanisms is the record of the East European countries—with their difficulties in participating in foreign trade and in even gaining admission into a trading framework. Within the Eastern bloc there are enormous difficulties connected with "planned trade." The effort to integrate different plans only multiplies problems that are already unmanageable. Market countries are not prepared to accord most-favored-nation treatment—or apply nondiscriminatory policies—to countries where competitiveness is not determined by efficiency but by government decree, and where the ground rules can change from one day to another. Government-administered pricing is difficult to accommodate in open trade.

The confusion caused by managed trade is conspicuous. It can be difficult for industries to see themselves outcompeted by someone more efficient, but such realities are—or have been—acceptable to capitalist governments because they are part of a trade process that leads to higher national income levels. Even industrialists and trade unions affected by the competition may acquiesce, since the advantages of being efficient will become apparent to them fairly quickly. Being outcompeted by a subsidized industry is a different matter. It seems unfair to those who suffer directly from it, and the distortions and uncertainties of the rules of this game make the net results negative.

Similarly, Atlantic and intra-European efforts to limit the losses of protectionism by means of a regionalization of free trade and a selective application of trade obstacles and escape clauses have caused strains. This is particularly evident in Europe. When the agonies of agricultural policies were extended to other product areas such as steel, the costs of trade diversion taxed the EEC spirit of cooperation. As a result, the common trade policy has shown signs of disintegration, and the regional free trade itself has been undermined by petty squabbles—over whether, for example, European-produced Japanese cars are European or Japanese. European-style agricultural policies are hardly manageable in a single sector, let alone in many. In Europe, as elsewhere, inward-looking integration has failed.

The Federation of Industry of the EEC countries has declared its disillusionment with the European Community: "Instead of concentrating action on those areas which would stimulate the growth and competitiveness of industry in the European Community and where new jobs can be created, the policies of the Community have been geared to protecting jobs in sectors that, in an open economy, have no growth prospects. . . . The European Community was not created to administer the decay of Europe." [42] The *Economist* of March 20-26, 1982, had a cover depicting the tombstone of the EEC, inscribed, "Born March 25, 1957, moribund March 25, 1982." What is now needed is not so much one "Grand Design" as many small designs—not so much a Grand Design to create one Market as the small designs necessary to make all the millions of markets, and especially the labor market, more market-like. These are the designs that must come first.

Asian-Pacific Responses to the Threat Notion

Increased protectionism in the established countries is an obvious threat to the Asian-Pacific countries. Countries that have not yet experimented fully with an outward orientation may simply respond by not undertaking reforms. Countries that are vigorous and are already deeply and successfully involved in international trade have some other interesting options for containing this threat.

Japan has the option of combating protectionism in other trading nations by means of a tenacious pursuit of high technology. With new technologies, Japan can develop a more resource-efficient and knowledge-based economy. New methods, new materials, and new energy sources will greatly reduce the need for imports of primary products. This will not only lower the risks of raw material diplomacy, but also reduce the fragility of Japan by diminishing its need for exports to cover the import bill. This would also make Japan's foreign trade less triangular. It is now characterized by large import surpluses vis-à-vis primary producers and large (and resented) export surpluses vis-à-vis manufacturing countries for the purpose of financing raw material imports. Japan's vulnerability to scapegoatism would decline if there were better bilateral balances in its foreign trade.

Furthermore, technological advances would both make Japan less dependent on imports of technology and provide trade-ins for use in the exchange of technological information. Although it was the high-tech advances of Japan that triggered American protectionism in trade and technology, these advances also promise an escape from the restrictions. In this context it is instructive to note how the Japanese "fifth generation" computer program, directed toward "artificial intelligence," is viewed by its organizers. In a research outline produced by the Institute for New Generation Computer

Technology, the following statement appears: "In Japan research and development has hitherto been aimed at catching up with technology of the United States and the advanced European nations. With Japanese technological achievements, however, the United States and advanced European nations have become wary of providing leading technologies, and we fear that the old style of catching-up research and development efforts will become more and more difficult. Leading and innovative research and development efforts are therefore necessary for a Japan that aims at prosperity through technology."[43]

Another, perhaps even more attractive advantage of technological sophistication is that advanced products for which there are few substitutes in other countries are less likely to encounter protectionist obstacles. Their successful marketing abroad does not result in any apparent displacement of labor. For instance, video tape recorders—which have a Japanese international market share of 97 percent—have fared better in trade policy than have, say, automobiles. In capital goods the run will be even smoother. The purchase of high technology producer goods may be a necessity for foreign companies if they, in turn, are to be competitive in other product lines.

A second, more conventional way of evading trade barriers is to engage in direct foreign investments, or "tariff factories." Japan has become heavily engaged in foreign investments not only as a means of reducing the fragility of a country so dependent on imports of primary products, but as a means of circumventing foreign trade obstacles. Japanese direct overseas investments have typically been concentrated in commerce, services, and resource development industries, in Asia and Latin America rather than in other advanced countries. Recently, however, the Japanese have increased their share of direct investment in manufacturing industries in advanced countries, for the specific purpose of gaining a better foothold in markets that are partly or wholly closed.[44] For the same reason, Korea and other countries are also displaying a kindling of interest in direct foreign investment.

A third means of coping with increasing protectionism is international trade policy. The Pacific home market has grown rapidly because of fast economic growth and a liberalization of the trade policies in the Pacific countries, and this market can play an even larger role. The sum of Asian-Pacific exports to other Asian-Pacific countries rose between 1960 and 1983 from U.S. $3.6 billion to U.S. $109 billion. Asian-Pacific exports to the United States in the same period rose from U.S. $2.2 billion to U.S. $86 billion.

The interdependencies in the Pacific have created an interest in regional cooperation. Since Kojima's first proposal for a free trade area in 1966,[45] there have been many suggestions and initiatives to create various councils, commissions, committees, and communities.[46] For a variety of reasons, the concrete results have not so far been dramatic. The heterogeneity of the region may make organized cooperation desirable, but also makes it difficult to formulate a clear mandate. The membership of any official organization would be unclear.

Should Latin America participate or not? Should the communist countries be invited in? Could Taiwan be a member if China was interested in joining? The towering position of Japan also causes some worries that she would dominate any organization. The United States could balance Japan, but then there would be greater apprehensions about possible domination by a "Gang of Two." The wide differences in levels of industrial sophistication also make it hard to formulate a common, equitable mandate. East Asia and the Pacific are a relatively unpromising environment for regionalism.

For these reasons, cooperation has begun on an unofficial level. Since 1967 the Pacific Basin Economic Council (PBEC) has been dedicated to Pacific business interests. It meets annually, and its aim is "to improve business environments, strengthen the business enterprise system, generate new business opportunities, create new business relationships, and increase trade and investment within the Pacific Basin area." Another forum for cooperation is the regular meetings of the Pacific Trade and Development Conference (PACTAD), set up in 1968 to bring together policy-oriented economists in the region for collaboration and consultation on Pacific economic policy research and thinking.[47] And since the early 1980's, a series of annual Pacific Economic Cooperation Conferences (PECC) have brought together government officials in a private capacity, as well as representatives of the academic and business sectors.

Australia, trying to establish a new identity, has taken a strong interest in Pacific cooperation. Before World War II, she was still an extension of Europe, but by the time Britain entered the EEC, Australia became both in fact and in her own view a Pacific country. In 1960 almost 30 percent of Australian exports went to Britain; by 1982 the figure was only about 5 percent. Meanwhile, the percentage of Australian exports going to Japan doubled, from about 15 to 30 percent.

But the country most interested in Pacific cooperation has been Japan. An imperial effort to widen the Japanese power base once led to disaster. Now, by means of trade and investment, the Japanese have managed to create something more profitable than even the dreamers on the Japanese general staff could have imagined—a creation, moreover, that also promises advantages to the countries once subjugated by those dreamers. Yet the memories of World War II have not been totally dispelled, and they have conditioned Japanese approaches to Pacific cooperation; having emerged as an economic superpower, Japan has had to avoid conveying the impression that history is somehow repeating itself. Japan has shown much activity but much restraint in her efforts toward Pacific integration. As Prime Minister Nakasone put it during a radio broadcast on November 20, 1984, "the question of

Japan's role [in Pacific cooperation] is a very delicate issue. We should remember that some people might still get worried about a return to the Greater East Asia Co-prosperity Sphere." The architectural attractions of blueprints have not been permitted to interfere with the construction work proceeding at the commercial level. There are some groups in Japan that look upon Asia as a refuge in case Japan is pushed back by the West. But a decisive restraining factor in Japan's Asian-Pacific trade policies is the fact that the region is not yet in a position to meet the economic needs of Japan, and will not be for a long time to come.[48]

On the subregional level, however, there is active government cooperation within the Association of Southeast Asian Nations (ASEAN). Devised as an economic organization, ASEAN has made some attempts at regional preferential tariff reductions. There have also been agreements on "ASEAN industries," but attempts at "agreed specialization" have (like all inward-looking integration) created centrifugal forces due to an unwillingness to assume the costs of trade diversion. ASEAN has had a slow start. It only became active many years after its birth, when the member countries were moved to act for foreign policy reasons—that is, to assume collective positions on Indo-China and the Vietnamese threat. ASEAN's economic activation, however, was only made possible by overall trade policies that had become more outward-oriented. ASEAN then became an instrument for more rapid deregulation of trade—not a mechanism for potentially divisive "collective self-reliance."

A continued liberalization of Asian-Pacific trade would facilitate trade and cooperation within the region. It would have the added advantage of permitting the Asian-Pacific countries to take a much more active role in international trade diplomacy and policymaking. Some of the Asian-Pacific countries maintain considerable trade obstacles. They could improve their own case in international trade diplomacy by moving more determinedly in the direction of free trade, and fully assuming their international obligations under the GATT rules. They would then be in a better position, both individually and collectively, to take economically significant actions against those who chose to discriminate against them. So far they have been divided in their approach, their position further weakened by the complicated political problems of the NICs. Although they are important actors in the world economy, they have accordingly found it convenient to accommodate and meekly accept a variety of "voluntary export restraints" and "orderly marketing agreements."[49]

The adoption of Asian-Pacific trade policies in conformity with GATT rules, and of a common stance against discriminatory trade policies, would be an important step toward halting the disintegration of the international trade policy system.[50] Japan in particular would be able to assume more active leadership in international policymaking by promoting efficient game rules. This leadership could prove as important to the world as her contribution to technology, innovation, and industry.

In spite of the enormous and largely self-inflicted adjustment difficulties of the Atlantic countries, the policies governing trade between those countries have weathered the strains rather better than the global trade commitments of the Atlantic countries. The main reason is that the risks of trade war in the Atlantic Basin are much more evenly divided, and the mutually agreed obligations more balanced. The internal political problems encountered by the established industrial countries in handling the adjustment pressures from Asian-Pacific competition would be greatly eased if the Asian-Pacific countries as a group could create the same balance of obligations vis-à-vis the Atlantic region as the United States and Europe have created for themselves. The negative effects of short-sighted protectionist measures would then become more apparent in the domestic political processes of the established countries. This may prove to be the best available method to preserve—and indeed to strengthen—the international trade policy framework that so greatly contributed to growth during the post-war decades and is now seriously threatened.

A Blessing in Being Found Out?

No country has an entitlement to prosperity. No region has special privileges. Historically inspired feelings of superiority cause misunderstandings, and the ensuing inflexibilities are not affordable. To use John Pinder's apt phrase, there must be "adjustment without tears."[51]

Asian-Pacific competition now underscores this reality. It demonstrates dramatically that staleness is not tolerable. This truth would have surfaced eventually in any case, but perhaps so slowly that much of the vigor needed to arrest the decline would have been spent in the interim. For the Atlantic region, and Europe in particular, the virtue of the demonstration effect of Pacific dynamism is that it exposes the need for vitality and the necessity to look for what can be achieved rather than for what can be maintained. It may be a blessing in disguise to be found out—to have weaknesses exposed—and to be opened up by the Asian-Pacific countries (shades of Commodore Perry) before stagnation makes change, policies for change, and attitudes favorable to change even more difficult to reinvent.

Reference Matter

Notes

Complete authors' names, titles, and publication data are given in the Bibliography, pp. 133-46.

Chapter One

1. See, for instance, Wu 1980. Wu gives the following numbers for minorities of ethnic Chinese: Malaysia, 3.7 million; Thailand, 3.5 million; Indonesia, 3.3 million; the Philippines, 0.6 million (Table 51, p. 133). The definitional problems of determining who precisely is an overseas Chinese are increasing, particularly in countries where intermarriage is common.

2. Mackintosh 1983: 8. Although three-quarters of the Soviet Union land area is in Asia and a third of it is east of Irkutsk, only 20 percent of the total population are of Asian origin and only 30 percent live in Asia.

3. Cook Islands (pop. 17 thousand), Fiji (pop. 646 thousand), Kiribati (pop. 59 thousand), Nauru (pop. 8 thousand), Solomon Islands (pop. 233 thousand), Tonga (pop. 99 thousand), Tuvalu (pop. 8 thousand), Vanuatu (pop. 120 thousand), and Western Samoa (pop. 157 thousand).

4. See, for instance, World Bank 1984: Table 3.5, p. 41.

Chapter Two

1. *Japan in the Year 2000*, pp. 105-6, 108, 149.

2. MITI 1980: 1, 10.

3. For instance, Jomo 1984, reviewed in *Far Eastern Economic Review*, Dec. 20, 1984.

4. Pacific Basin Cooperation Study Group 1980: 7. See also Donowaki 1981. Donowaki was a member of the study group.

5. *Japan in the Year 2000*, pp. 109-10.

6. Ibid.: 18.

7. On Confucianism, see, for instance, Han Seung Soo, "Of Economic Success and Confucianism," *Far Eastern Economic Review*, Dec. 20, 1984; on the Japanese ethos, Morishima 1982; on Japanese industrial policy, Johnson 1982.

8. In his writings on the sociology of religion Max Weber attributed northwest European growth to a wide range of characteristics of Protestantism, rather than just to its much-heralded work ethic. Discussing Con-

fucianism, he concluded that the mental attitudes of Confucianism had been a major factor in preventing the emergence of modern capitalism in China (Weber 1951).

9. Wu 1980, 1983. In spite of some initial discrimination, the Chinese minority has also been successful in the United States. The average income of ethnic Chinese born in the United States is higher than the U.S. average. If education is held constant, Chinese-Americans have the same earnings as white Americans (Chiswick 1983).

10. See, for instance, Johnson 1982; Magaziner and Reich 1982.

11. U.S. Council of Economic Advisers 1984: 99.

12. For a fact-finding exposition of Japanese industrial policy, see U.S. International Trade Commission 1983. For an evaluation of Japanese industrial policy, see Saxonhouse 1983a; Okimoto 1984; Trezise 1983; Schultze 1983; U.S. Council of Economic Advisers 1984: ch. 3. For a good general discussion of the problems of industrial policy, see Lindbeck 1981. In his careful analysis of the various industrial policies of Japan, Okimoto (1984: 78) concludes: "There is no alchemy involved in MITI's 'secret' formula for successful industrial policy. Most of its policies can be found on any standard list used by states seeking to promote their hi tech industries."

13. Schultze 1983: 7.

14. See, for instance, Hong 1984b.

15. World Bank 1983a: 62.

16. Johnson 1982: 10. In a similar vein, Herman Kahn writes (1970: 88-89): "The situation in Japan is very different from that in the United States. Probably more than 50 percent of all Japanese government officials devote their time to improving the prospects of business. However, one would conjecture that in the United States more than 50 percent of all government officials devote their time to almost the opposite task—many of them to sponsoring groups with grudges against the business system and the establishment, or groups that are antibusiness, antieconomic growth, anticapitalist, and even antirationalist, at least from the economic point of view."

17. See, for instance, Hong 1984b.

18. The Korean savings ratio has long been relatively small, but rates of interest were kept low by heavy interference with the credit and capital markets in order to implement industrial policies. See Hong 1984b.

19. See, for instance, on Taiwan, Scitovsky 1982; Galenson 1979; Kuo, Ranis, and Fei 1981; Lee and Liang 1982; Kuo 1983. On Korea, Scitovsky 1982; Krueger 1979; Mason 1980; Westphal and Kim 1982. On Singapore, Tan and Hock 1982. On Hong Kong, Chen 1979; Rabushka 1979; Lin and Ho 1981. On Japan, Patrick and Rosovsky 1976.

20. There have been major research projects into these policy experiences. Studies have been organized through OECD (see Little, Scitovsky, and Scott 1970), the World Bank (see, for instance, Balassa 1977, 1981a), and the National Bureau of Economic Research (see Krueger 1978; Bhagwati 1978). See also Little 1982.

21. Balassa 1981a: 16-17.
22. See Balassa 1981b.
23. Rosenberg and Birdzell 1985: 301.
24. Ibid.: 9.
25. For a recent instance, see Rabushka 1984.
26. Friedman and Friedman 1980: 57.
27. White 1984: 87.
28. See, for instance, Vogel 1979, on emulation and inspiration in general; Weitzman 1984, on macroeconomic reform; Johnson 1982, on industrial policy; Ouchi 1981 and Pascale and Athos 1981, on management techniques; Linder 1983, on welfare policies; and White 1984, on education. Some of these Japanese attractions were originally imported from the West, but have been put to systematic and good use in Japan.
29. On some of the early hopes and disappointments, see Lim 1974.
30. Krueger 1984: 6, 8.
31. The point is made forcefully by Keesing (1979: 1).
32. Havrylyshyn and Alikani 1982. Number one on this list of the fastest-growing exporters of manufactures is Sri Lanka, which was influenced by Singapore's example in particular in successfully reorienting its economic policies during the 1970's. The other countries are Cyprus (2), Peru (5), Jordan (6), Uruguay (7), Tunisia (9), the Philippines (10), Colombia (11), and Morocco (12).
33. Keesing 1979: v, 149. Keesing mentions Sri Lanka and India as two countries where this reorientation has been taking place. In November 1983, the government of Pakistan ran a four-page advertisement in the *Economist* describing the ambitions of its sixth five-year plan: "Under the Fifth Plan the government made a start at improving public-private sector relations by beginning the process of deregulating the economy. . . . The Sixth Plan intends going much further. . . . The government seeks to create a more efficient, internationally competitive economy."
34. Lal 1983.
35. The foremost dissenter on aid is P. T. Bauer (1976, 1981). See also Brunner 1978; Schultz 1981; Krauss 1983; and even Myrdal 1980. Donald Keesing (1979: 148) specifically argues that "the foreign exchange needs of each economy [Taiwan's and Korea's], especially once U.S. aid was cut back, dictated a protrade policy." For some years, the rising aid scepticism has been noted and discussed by the OECD Development Assistance Committee (e.g., OECD 1981).
36. Castro 1980: 65.
37. Pacific Basin Cooperation Study Group 1980: 21.
38. Harding 1984: 3. According to the *Financial Times* for March 6, 1984, figures just then released by China's State Council showed that in 1978 there were only 140,000 people engaged in private businesses throughout China; there were now 7.5 million. Between 1978 and 1982, China gained 1.5 million retail stores, 628,000 restaurants and food shops (a fourfold increase), and 597,000 service trade shops. About 80 percent of all the new

businesses were privately owned. Hao Haifeng, director of the state department responsible for managing private economic activity, was quoted as saying: "During those terrible ten years of the Cultural Revolution (1966-76), these private businesses were regarded as capitalist tails that should be cut off. . . . But history has given us a very profound lesson. We see that a uniform national economy cannot bring prosperity to China." It may be added that the reforms in agriculture are the most extensive ones and that the figures in the *Financial Times* article do not cover this sector.

39. See Brus 1980; Knaack 1981; Solinger 1981; Balassa 1982c; Cheung 1982; Knight 1983; Harding 1984; and the various contributions to *China Under the Four Modernizations* (Joint Economic Committee 1982).

40. A quotation from Zhou Bin (1982: 5), researcher at the Chinese Academy of Social Sciences, illustrates this difficulty: "China is a socialist country, and research systems differ from those of most other countries. When dealing with more serious questions such as practical politics or international problems, researchers generally approach their work with caution. They frequently seek the opinions of others within their group and will only risk publicly announcing their findings when they feel a certain degree of confidence."

41. Johnson 1982: viii.

42. Davie and Carver 1982: 28. It should be emphasized that when Chinese economists write something, they are expressing officially approved opinion, not just individual idiosyncrasies.

43. Zhou Bin 1982.

44. Nanto 1982: 110.

45. Speech appearing in a document dated Sept. 4, 1979, and labeled "materials for study" in a publication from the State Councils Secretariat. Professor Yuan-li Wu of Hoover Institution, Stanford, has brought my attention to Yu Qiu-li's speech and made the translation. At the time he gave the speech, Yu Qiu-li was a member of the Polit Bureau of the Central Committee, Vice Premier, and Chairman of the Planning Commission.

46. Lipset 1984: 21. Lipset notes a considerable effort to stimulate competition. He describes China as macrocommunist and microcapitalist. The latter aspect, he argues, "is reflected in the emphasis on and pride in the growth of 'free markets'" (ibid.: 6).

47. Huan Hsiang 1983: 1.

48. Data from IMF 1963, 1984, and U.N. 1984.

49. Joy Barson (1981) quotes various Chinese officials in support of the view that the special economic zones are not just duty-free enclaves to increase exports, but experiments to open regions up in order to bring in Western capital and management and to modernize. (Current issues of the *Far Eastern Economic Review* can be consulted for information on these zones.) The zones offer special concessions, including tax holidays for foreign companies that enter joint ventures or make solitary investments. The biggest zone is Shenzhen, which borders Hong Kong. The *Far Eastern Economic Review* of November 10, 1983, has a report on Arnold Palmer open-

ing a golf course, designed by him and financed by Hong Kong Chinese interests, in the Guangdong province near Canton. According to the *Financial Times* of March 29, 1984, Deng Xiaoping informed Japanese Prime Minister Nakasone that China intended to open more of these zones. In the same report, a senior government official is quoted as saying that "the success of existing zones had proved the correctness of China's policies of opening to the West." There are also fourteen coastal cities that have been authorized to establish direct foreign investment and trade links (a privilege similar to that granted in 1980 to the special economic zones). The October 11, 1984, issue of the *Far Eastern Economic Review* carries an article on one of these, the Dalian port: "Zone officials told the *Review* that they had been taking advice from businessmen from Hong Kong, Singapore, Thailand and Japan." Doubts remain, however, about China's ability to liberalize and provide stable enough game rules to make the zones attractive.

50. These attempts receive continuous coverage in *Far Eastern Economic Review* and the international financial press.

51. *Far Eastern Economic Review*, Dec. 8, 1983, p. 16.

52. Baran 1957: 163-64, 249.

53. Little 1982: 219.

54. For careful empirical discussions of these arguments (arguments repeated in, for instance, the Brandt reports, 1980 and 1983), see Landes 1977; Bhagwati 1977; Corden 1979; Spraos 1980; Bauer 1981; Trade Policy Research Centre 1981; Little 1982. The particular argument Landes overthrows is the neo-Marxist assertion that the center managed its growth only by importing essentials from the periphery at marauding prices. In fact, during its long takeoff period, Europe imported mainly luxuries like spices, sugar, and tobacco. On this point, see also Lewis 1978: 30.

55. Zagoria 1982: 4.

56. Scalapino 1982: 61.

57. See Vasey and Viksnins 1976. Singapore's Foreign Minister Rajaratnam expounded on this point in a speech some years after the end of the Vietnam War.

58. A remarkable alliance of this type is pointed out by the Indian economist Deepak Lal. He reports on new research showing that the difficulties of the Indian textile industry in the late nineteenth century were due partly to factory acts that made low-productivity Indian labor uncompetitive. The acts were pushed through by a combination of philanthropists and manufacturers in the United Kingdom. "As is usual in such alliances," says Lal, "the selfish English protectionist interest was better served by this legislation than the altruism of the philanthropists." Lal goes on to point out that today "a similar pauper-labor argument is being resurrected to force Third World governments to grant their labor the same rights, including a common worldwide minimum wage, as those accorded to workers in OECD countries" (Lal 1983: 86).

59. Streeten 1982: 166.

60. Myers 1983: 537.

61. I. M. D. Little, quoted in Lal 1983: 45 from an ILO paper.

62. In his classic study of economic growth and income inequality, Kuznets (1955) drew this conclusion from the experiences of the advanced countries and data from LDCs. Other economists have also found that income disparities must apparently worsen before they can improve (e.g., Paukert 1973; Adelman and Morris 1973). For a recent study of the problem of income distribution comparisons and income distribution changes in many developing countries, see Fields 1980.

63. On income distribution in Korea, see Mason et al. 1980: ch. 12. Even allowing for the weaknesses of the statistical material, "there is no reason to challenge the conclusion [made in other studies] that the degree of income inequality in Korea is substantially less than that existing in many other less-developed countries. . . . Korea has been hailed as a prime example of how growth can be achieved with equity" (ibid.: 408). During the 1970's distributional equity deteriorated in Korea.

64. Pranab K. Bardhan had this to say about the situation in India (Chenery et al. 1974: 255-56): "Removal of social and economic injustices and assurance of minimum levels of living have been among the most important Directive Principles laid down in the Indian Constitution. Right from the inception of planning these have been among the most prominent explicitly stated objectives of government economic policy. In the last two decades or more, a whole host of policy measures . . . had been taken toward achieving these objectives. Yet, by most accounts, about half of the population continues to live in abject poverty, and the distribution of income, wealth, and economic power continues to be extremely unequal."

65. Rao and Ramakrishnan 1976. The Gini coefficients are .498 for 1966 and .448 for 1975.

66. See Kuo 1983: ch. 6; Kuo, Ranis, and Fei 1981; Fei, Ranis, and Kuo 1979; Kuznets 1979; Chenery et al. 1974.

67. Rawski 1982: 25-26. See also Vermeer 1982.

68. "Now . . . that, socially, the troubles of the West European-type welfare society are becoming clear, an economic society of the Western type can no longer be a model for Japan" (*Japan in the Year 2000*, p. 18).

69. The problems of transition have been widely discussed. See, for instance, Krueger 1978, 1981b; Keesing 1979; Little 1982: 144ff.

70. Cline 1982b; Streeten 1982.

71. For data on the small share of imports from LDCs in apparent consumption in industrial countries, see UNCTAD 1983b.

72. Balassa 1981a; Henderson 1982; Havrylyshyn and Civan 1983.

73. Riedel 1983: 38.

74. Even with LDC protectionism at its present level, this kind of intra-LDC trade has increased substantially. See, for instance, Havrylyshyn and Wolf 1981, 1983a,b.

75. See, for instance, Boltho 1982; Dahrendorf 1982; and Carli 1983.

76. Stern 1977: 133.

77. *Japan in the Year 2000*, pp. 28-29.

78. Hanabusa 1979: 98.

79. Kikuchi 1983. Europe does not figure much in this book, except anecdotally. Speaking of the willpower he regards as "the driving force behind Japan's rapid progress," Kikuchi recounts the following episode: "I can remember visiting Paris in 1981 and having dinner with a French laboratory director at Le Galion, a floating restaurant on the Seine. My partner laughed when I asked if we would go back to his labs for our afternoon talk. 'Don't be in such a hurry,' he said. 'They'll be bringing the cheese and the brandy next.' A little concerned lest he be laughing at me, instead of with me, I hastily reconsidered what I had just said. But I still felt some lingering discontent. Was it really all right to spend so much time at lunch? Generally speaking, European culture is very calm and relaxed, and I, for one, am certainly in no position to pass judgment on whether it is good or bad" (p. 97).

80. Feigenbaum and McCorduck 1983: 186.

Chapter Three

1. Hall 1957: 716-17.

2. See Lach 1965; Darling 1980; Kohn 1934. On the transfer of technology from East to West, see the monumental work by Needham and Ling (1954-70).

3. Fairbank, Reischauer, and Craig 1973: 243.

4. See Li 1965: 281-89. "That Cheng Ho's expeditions brought back nothing remarkable except such curiosities as ostriches, zebras, and giraffes further convinced them that while foreigners depended upon China for the improvement of their livelihood, China had nothing to gain in trading with foreigners. This belief was strengthened in a later period by the insistence of Western Europeans on opening China to trade." (Ibid.: 288.)

5. Landes 1977: 4.

6. Greenberg 1951: 1.

7. Thompson, Stanley, and Perry 1981: 33.

8. From the very beginning, it was illegal to import opium into China. Regulations were complicated, however, because these forbidden imports "suited the purposes of local Chinese officials, who used [their] illegality as a pretext for collecting bribes from would-be importers" (Thompson, Stanley, and Perry 1981: 35).

9. Lach 1965, vol. 1: xiii.

10. Hofheinz and Calder 1982: 5.

11. The Asian-Pacific share of Chinese exports is very high. The reexports going through Hong Kong, however, introduce some statistical uncertainties, and probably exaggerate the reported exports to the Asian-Pacific market.

12. IMF 1983 reports receipts of workers' remittances in the amount of SDR 735 million in 1982 for the Philippines and SDR 106 million for Korea. For the same year, the World Bank (1983a) reports U.S. $616 million in receipts of workers' remittances for Thailand, $240 million for the Philippines, and $126 million for Korea. The discrepancies indicate that the data are unreliable. They probably understate, rather than overstate, the earnings of guest workers.

13. The net current account for all countries in the world should sum to zero. There are statistical defects, however. For instance, for 1979 there was an aggregate deficit of U.S. $5 billion. In 1980 the aggregate deficit was U.S. $1 billion; in 1981, U.S. $51 billion; in 1982, U.S. $91 billion; and in 1983, U.S. $70 billion (IMF 1984: Table 7, p. 23). In all probability, the errors are rather in the statistics for trade in services than for trade in goods, and the Asian-Pacific countries are proportionally less engaged in trade in services than the United States and Western Europe. If Asian-Pacific countries were to have a proportional share of understated exports and overstated imports of goods and services, however, their net current account position would have to be corrected by an addition of perhaps U.S. $25 billion for the four-year period 1979-82.

14. For Japanese direct foreign investment, see Sekiguchi 1982; Kojima 1978; and Ozawa 1979.

15. Japan External Trade Organization 1984: 12.

16. United States-Japan macroeconomic interaction, the most important bilateral relationship, is treated by, for example, Saxonhouse 1982a; Krause and Sekiguchi 1980: chs. 8-9; Destler and Mitsuyu, in Destler and Sato 1982.

17. For a general review and analysis of the content of Japanese R&D trends, see Okimoto and Saxonhouse 1983.

18. For a discussion of Japanese trade in technology and an evaluation of the empirical material on this trade, see, for instance, Peck and Tamura in Patrick and Rosovsky 1976; Lynn 1983; Ozawa 1983.

19. See, for instance, Miller 1983a,b.

Chapter Four

1. The following list of official U.S. documents dealing with United States-Japan trade problems illustrates both the large volume of the discussions and the positions taken by representatives of these three groups: (1) Joint Economic Committee, (a) *Hearing on U.S.-Japan Trade Relations*, Oct. 10, 1979, (b) *Hearings on U.S.-Japan Economic Relations*, June 19, July 9, 13, 1981 (Subcommittee on International Trade, Finance, and Security Economics); (2) Senate, (a) Select Committee on Small Business, *Hearing on Impact of Non-Tariff Barriers on the Ability of Small Business to Export to Japan*, June 25, 1980, (b) Committee on Foreign Relations, *Hearing on U.S. Trade Relations with Japan*, Sept. 14, 1982; (3) House of Rep-

resentatives, (a) Committee on Foreign Affairs (Subcommittee on Asian and Pacific Affairs), *Hearings on U.S.-Japan Relations*, Mar. 1, 3, 9, 17, 24, Apr. 27, June 2, 15, Aug. 4, 1982, (b) Committee on Ways and Means (Subcommittee on Trade), *United States-Japan Trade Report* (by a task force established by the Subcommittee), Sept. 5, 1980, *Hearings on Trade with Japan*, Aug. 26, Sept. 18, 1980, and *Hearings on U.S.-Japan Trade Relations*, Mar. 10, Apr. 21, 26, 1983; (4) *Report of the Japan-United States Economic Relations Group*, prepared for the President of the United States and the Prime Minister of Japan, Jan. 1981, with a *Supplementary Report*, Oct. 1981, and with an *Appendix to the Report of the Japan-U.S. Economic Relations Group*, Apr. 1981. The *Congressional Information Service Index* lists a wealth of additional congressional material on United States-Japan issues.

Many EEC documents also report on trade with Japan. See, for example, the *Denman Report* (1979), the *Five Point Plan* (1980), and "Japan and the European Communities: A Stocktaking" (I/216/84-EN, Apr. 1984).

In Tokyo the constant ministerial visits and missions of government representatives, industrialists, and trade unionists from the United States, the European countries, and the EEC Commission to discuss trade problems receive daily coverage in the Japanese newspapers. (There is also a steady reverse flow of goodwill missions from Japan to the Western countries.)

For a study with a somewhat different perspective from my own, see Krause 1982, on shaping U.S. trade policies toward ASEAN countries in order to meet the Japanese challenge.

2. Hofheinz and Calder 1982: 12-13.

3. See, for instance, Hanabusa 1979; Hanson and Roehl 1980; Hollerman 1980; Tasca 1980; Baranson 1981; Destler and Sato 1982; Tsoukalis and White 1982; Yamamura 1982. These books discuss trade relations with Japan.

4. Rosenberg 1982: 254.

5. See Okimoto and Saxonhouse 1983: 10, 57, 62; Feigenbaum and MacCorduck 1983: 217.

6. On this technological protectionism, see, for instance, Saxonhouse 1983a; Okimoto and Saxonhouse 1983: 26, 53.

7. One sometimes hears the term "goatability" used to describe this phenomenon. I first encountered the term (evidently invented in Japan) in a conversation with Saburo Okita. It was used in an article in the *New York Times* on Nov. 7, 1983.

8. See Patterson 1966: 273-300. See esp. p. 275.

9. Hubbard 1935: 107.

10. Lawrence 1984. See also Bergsten 1982, on the effects of misaligned exchange rates on deindustrialization fears.

11. See OECD 1979b: Annex II; OECD 1981. See also Krueger 1980b; Kierzkowski 1980.

12. OECD 1979b: 6.

13. Ibid.: 94.

14. Ibid.: 12. The NIC group referred to in the OECD study includes some non-Asian countries, but this does not affect the relevance of the study's conclusions in the present context.

15. Good reviews of trade policy developments are to be found in Anjaria et al. 1981, 1982. For recent discussions of the (negative) economic results of the protectionist revival among Western industrial countries, see, for instance, Lal 1982; Hindley and Nicolaides 1983; Corden 1974.

16. For Japanese trade policies, see Saxonhouse 1983a.

17. Charcoal briquettes and four leather-product categories.

18. It is reasonably easy to calculate the incidence of national tariff levels, but difficult even to obtain information on all the nontariff trade barriers (NTBs). The GATT does not maintain an inventory of all these restrictions and information is hard to extract from much of the relevant national legislation.

19. Wilkinson 1981.

20. Japan-United States 1981.

21. Saxonhouse 1982b, 1983b.

22. It should be noted, however, that some of these neighboring countries have large import deficits in their trade with Japan, so that it may seem advantageous for them to join the chorus—and hope that pressures on the Japanese by other countries will not result in agreements that damage their own position. Australia, which actually has an export surplus vis-à-vis Japan, is concerned lest U.S. attacks on Japanese agricultural protectionism yield agreements giving U.S. agricultural interests a still more advantageous position in Japan than they already enjoy in comparison with Australian interests.

23. U.S. Council of Economic Advisers 1984: 66.

24. Ibid.: 66-67.

25. U.S. International Trade Commission 1983: 1.

26. Ibid.: 4.

27. U.S. Council of Economic Advisers 1984: 88, 99.

28. National Science Board 1983: 200.

29. Saxonhouse 1983a: 270. A similar conclusion is drawn in Okimoto 1984 and in Krugman 1984.

30. Saxonhouse 1983a: 268.

31. Ibid.: 267. For a list of such measures taken by the Japanese, see Okimoto and Saxonhouse 1983: 60-61.

32. For an exposition of this process as a cause of the decline of nations, see Olson 1982.

33. *The Economist,* Nov. 24, 1984, p. 99. *Newsweek* of Apr. 9, 1984, also reflected the prevailing apprehensions in a lengthy special report entitled "The Decline of Europe."

34. OECD 1982b: 12.

35. Lawrence 1984: 35.

36. On labor market changes of this type, see Franco Bernabe in Boltho 1982.

37. CEC 1982: 14.

38. CEC 1983: 11, 12, 14.

39. CEC 1984: 42.

40. Boltho 1982; Dahrendorf 1982; Emerson 1984.

41. Waelbroeck 1983: 413, 417.

42. Carli 1983: 446.

43. ICOT 1982: 2-3.

44. Economic Planning Agency 1984: 62-69.

45. For a presentation of the original ideas in book form, see Kojima 1971.

46. For a recent study, see Oborne and Fourt 1983. The Japan Center for International Exchange has a list of proposals, projects, and organizations concerned with Pacific cooperation. On the history of efforts at cooperation in the Pacific, see, for instance, Trade Policy Research Centre 1983: ch. 4.

47. See Patrick and Drysdale 1983.

48. For a discussion of these problems, see Morrison and Sato 1984.

49. Yoffie and Keohane (1981) and Yoffie (1983) analyze the strategies of the new industrial countries in heading off protectionism by submission.

50. For a forceful presentation of similar arguments, see Trade Policy Research Centre 1983; Dunn 1983; Kim Jae-ik 1983.

51. See Pinder in Tsoukalis and White 1982.

Bibliography

Adelman, Irma, and Cynthia Taft Morris. 1973. *Economic Growth and Social Equity in Developing Countries*. Stanford, Calif.

Anjaria, S. J., et al. 1981. *Trade Policy Developments in Industrial Countries*. International Monetary Fund, Occasional Papers no. 5, Washington, D.C.

――――. 1982. *Developments in International Trade Policy*. International Monetary Fund, Occasional Papers no. 16, Washington, D.C.

Asian Development Bank. 1984. *Key Indicators of Developing Member Countries of ADB*. Manila.

Balassa, Bela. 1977. *Policy Reform in Developing Countries*. Oxford and New York.

――――. 1978a. "Export Incentives and Export Performance in Developing Countries: A Comparative Analysis," *Weltwirtschaftliches Archiv*, 1: 24-61.

――――. 1978b. "Exports and Economic Growth: Further Evidence," *Journal of Development Economics*, June, pp. 181-89.

――――. 1980. *The Process of Industrial Development and Alternative Development Strategies*. Princeton, N.J.

――――. 1981a. *The Newly Industrializing Countries in the World Economy*. New York.

――――. 1981b. "The Newly Industrialized Countries After the Oil Crisis," *Weltwirtschaftliches Archiv*, 1: 142-94.

――――. 1982a. *Policy Responses to External Shocks in Sub-Saharan African Countries*. World Bank Development Research Department Report, no. 42, Washington, D.C.

――――. 1982b. "Structural Adjustment Policies in Developing Countries," *World Development*, 1: 22-38.

――――. 1982c. "Economic Reform in China," *Banca Nazionale del Lavoro Quarterly Review*, Sept., pp. 307-33.

Balassa, Bela, et al. 1982. *Development Strategies in Semi-Industrial Economies*. Baltimore.

Baldwin, Robert. 1969. "The Case Against Infant-Industry Protection," *Journal of Political Economy*, May-June, pp. 295-305.

————. 1981. "U.S. Political Pressures Against Adjustment to Greater Imports." In Hong and Krause 1981, pp. 515-50.

Baran, P. A. 1957. *The Political Economy of Growth*. New York.

Baranson, Jack. 1981. *The Japanese Challenge to U.S. Industry*. Lexington, Mass.

Barson, Joy. 1981. "Special Economic Zones in the People's Republic of China," *China-International Business*, 5: 461-94.

Bauer, P. T. 1976. *Dissent on Development*. Rev. Ed. Cambridge, Mass.

————. 1981. *Equality, the Third World and Economic Delusion*. Cambridge, Mass.

Bergsten, Fred C. 1982. "What to Do About the U.S.-Japan Economic Conflict," *Foreign Affairs*, Summer, pp. 1059-75.

Bergsten, Fred C., and William R. Cline. 1982. *Trade Policy in the 1980's*. Inst. for International Economics, Washington, D.C.

Bhagwati, Jagdish. 1977. *The New International Economic Order: The North-South Debate*. Cambridge, Mass.

————. 1978. *Anatomy and Consequences of Exchange Control Regimes*. Cambridge, Mass.

————, ed. 1982. *Import Competition and Response*. Chicago.

Black, John, and Brian Hindley, eds. 1980. *Current Issues in Commercial Policy and Diplomacy*. Trade Policy Research Centre, London.

Boltho, A., ed. 1982. *The European Economy: Growth and Crisis*. New York.

Bradford, Colin I. 1981. "ADCs' Manufactured Export Growth and OECD Adjustment." In Hong and Krause 1981, pp. 476-506.

Brandt Commission. 1983. *Common Crisis–North-South: Cooperation for World Recovery*. London.

Brandt Report. 1980. *North-South–a Programme for Survival*. The Report of the Independent Commission on International Development Issues Under the Chairmanship of Willy Brandt. London.

Brunner, Karl, ed. 1978. *The First World and the Third World*. New York.

Brus, Wlodzimierz. 1980. "Problems of the Incipient Reform of the Economic System in the People's Republic of China." Background paper for the World Bank, Oxford.

Carli, Guido. 1983. "Disillusion with the European Community in Business Circles," *World Economy*, Dec., pp. 445-47.

Castro, Amado. 1980. "ASEAN Economic Co-operation." In Garnaut 1980, pp. 53-65.

CEC (Commission of the European Communities). 1982. *Annual Economic Report 1982-83*. Brussels.

————. 1983. *Annual Economic Report 1983-84*. Brussels.

————. 1984. *Annual Economic Report 1984-85*. Brussels.

Chen, Edward. 1979. *Hyper-Growth in Asian Economies*. London.

Chenery, Hollis B. 1961. "Comparative Advantage and Development Policy," *American Economic Review*, Mar., pp. 18-51.

————, et al. 1974. *Redistribution with Growth*. New York.

Cheung, Steven N. S. 1982. *Will China Go Capitalist?* Inst. of Economic Affairs, London.

Chiswick, Berry R. 1983. "An Analysis of the Earnings and Employment of Asian-American Minorities," *Journal of Labor Economics*, Apr., pp. 197-214.

CIA. 1984. *Handbook of Economic Statistics*. Washington, D.C.

Cline, William R., ed. 1979. *Policy Alternatives for a New International Economic Order*. New York.

————. 1982a. *"Reciprocity": A New Approach to World Trade Policy?* Inst. of International Economics, Washington, D.C.

————. 1982b. "Can the East-Asian Model of Development Be Generalized?" *World Development*, Feb., pp. 81-99.

————, ed. 1983. *Trade Policy in the 1980's*. Inst. for International Economics, Washington, D.C.

Cline, William R., and Sidney Weintraub, eds. 1981. *Economic Stabilization in Developing Countries*. Brookings Institution, Washington, D.C.

Cooper, Richard N. 1980. *The Economics of Interdependence: Economic Policy in the Atlantic Community*. New York.

Corbet, Hugh, ed. 1970. *Trade Strategy and the Asian-Pacific Region*. London.

Corden, W. M. 1971. *The Theory of Protection*. Oxford.

————. 1974. *Trade Policy and Economic Welfare*. Oxford.

————. 1979. *The Nieo Proposals: A Cool Look*. Trade Policy Research Centre, London.

Dahrendorf, Ralf, ed. 1982. *Europe's Economy in Crisis*. New York.

Darling, Frank C. 1980. *The Westernization of Asia: A Comparative Political Analysis*. Cambridge, Mass.

Davie, John L., and Dean W. Carver. 1982. "China's International Trade and Finance." In *China Under the Four Modernizations: Selected Papers Submitted to the Joint Economic Committee, Congress of the United States*, Aug. 13, pp. 19-47. Washington, D.C.

Denison, E., and W. K. Chung. 1976. *How Japan's Economy Grew So Fast*. Brookings Institution, Washington, D.C.

Dernberger, Robert F. 1982. "The Chinese Search for the Path of Self-Sustained Growth in the 1980's: An Assessment." In *China Under the Four Modernizations: Selected Papers Submitted to the Joint Economic Committee, Congress of the United States*, Aug. 13, pp. 19-76. Washington, D.C.

Destler, I. M., and Hideo Sato, eds. 1982. *Coping with U.S.-Japanese Economic Conflicts*. Lexington, Mass.

Donowaki, Mitsuro. 1981. "The Pacific Basin Community: The Evolution of a Concept," *Speaking of Japan*, Mar., pp. 23-32.

Dunn, Lydia. 1983. "Scope for Asian-Pacific Action of Protectionism," *Asia-Pacific Community*, Fall, pp. 7-19.

The Economist. 1982. "Is Free Trade Dead?" Dec. 25, pp. 75-91.
———. 1984. "Europe's Technology Gap," Nov. 24, pp. 99-110.
The Economist Intelligence Unit (EIU). 1983. *Towards the Pacific Century: Economic Development in the Pacific Basin.* EIU Special Report no. 137, London.
Emerson, Michael. 1984. *Europe's Stagflation: Causes and Cures.* Commission of the European Communities, Brussels.
Fairbank, John K., Edwin O. Reischauer, and Albert M. Craig. 1973. *East Asia, Tradition and Transformation.* Boston.
Far Eastern Economic Review. 1984. *Asia Yearbook.* Hong Kong.
Fei, John C. H., Gustav Ranis, and Shirley W. Y. Kuo. 1979. *Growth with Equity: The Taiwan Case.* London.
Feigenbaum, Edward A., and Pamela McCorduck. 1983. *The Fifth Generation, Artificial Intelligence and Japan's Computer Challenge to the World.* Reading, Mass.
Fields, G. S. 1980. *Poverty, Inequality and Development.* Cambridge, Eng.
Findlay, Ronald. 1980. In Garnaut 1980, pp. 45-46.
Finger, J. M. 1981. *Industrial Country Policy and Adjustment to Imports from Developing Countries.* World Bank Staff Working Paper no. 470, Washington, D.C.
Frank, Isaiah. 1979. *The "Graduation" Issue in Trade Policy Toward LDCs.* World Bank Staff Working Paper no. 334, Washington, D.C.
———. 1981. *Trade Policy Issues for the Developing Countries in the 1980's.* World Bank Staff Working Paper no. 478, Washington, D.C.
French-Davis, Ricardo. 1980. In Garnaut 1980, pp. 46-49.
Friedman, Milton, and Rose Friedman. 1980. *Free to Choose.* New York.
Galenson, Walter, ed. 1979. *Economic Growth and Structural Change in Taiwan.* Ithaca, N.Y.
Garnaut, Ross, ed. 1980. *ASEAN in a Changing Pacific and World Economy.* Canberra.
GATT (General Agreement on Tariffs and Trade). 1984. *International Trade 1983/84.* Geneva.
Gibney, Frank. 1983. "Patterns of Asia Modernization." Paper read at a Hudson Research Europe conference, Apr. 23, New York. Mimeo.
Goh, Keng Swee. 1983. "Public Administration and Economic Development in LDCs." Fourth Harry G. Johnson Memorial Lecture, Trade Policy Research Centre, London. Mimeo.
Greenberg, Michael. 1951. *British Trade and the Opening of China 1800-1842.* Cambridge, Eng.
Gregory, Gene. 1982. *The Japanese Propensity for Innovation: Electronics.* Business Series no. 86, Sophia University, Inst. of Comparative Culture, Tokyo.
Hall, A. R. 1957. "Epilogue: The Rise of the West." In *A History of Technology,* Vol. 3, ed. Charles Singer, et al. Oxford.
Hanabusa, Masamichi. 1979. *Trade Problems Between Japan and Western Europe.* New York.

Hanson, Kermit O., and T. W. Roehl, eds. 1980. *The U.S. and the Pacific Economy in the 1980's.* Indianapolis.

Harding, Harry. 1984. "The Transformation of China," *The Brookings Review*, Spring, pp. 3-7.

Havrylyshyn, Oli. 1983. "The Increasing Integration of Newly Industrializing Countries in World Trade." Mimeo, the World Bank, Washington, D.C.

Havrylyshyn, Oli, and I. Alikani. 1982. "Is There Cause for Export Optimism? An Inquiry into the Existence of a Second Generation of Successful Exporters," *Weltwirtschaftliches Archiv* 4: 651-61.

Havrylyshyn, Oli, and E. Civan. 1982a. *Intra-Industry Trade Among Developing Countries.* World Bank Division Working Paper no. 1982-6, Washington, D.C.

———. 1982b. *Determinants of Intra-Industry Trade in Developing and Industrial Countries: A Cross-Country Regression Analysis.* World Bank Division Working Paper no. 1982-7, Washington, D.C.

———. 1983. "Intra-Industry Trade and the Stage of Development." In *Intra-Industry Trade*, ed. P. K. M. Thorokan. New York.

Havrylyshyn, Oli, and Martin Wolf. 1981. *Trade Among Developing Countries: Theory, Policy Issues, and Principal Trends.* World Bank Division Working Paper no. 1981-2, Washington, D.C.

———. 1983a. "Recent Trends in Trade Among Developing Countries," *European Economic Review* 21: 333-62.

———. 1983b. "Collective Self-Reliance as a Trade Policy for Developing Countries: A Critique." Mimeo, Trade Policy Research Centre, London.

Henderson, P. D. 1982. "Trade Policies and 'Strategies'—Case for Liberal Approach," *World Economy*, Nov., pp. 291-302.

Hindley, Brian, and Eri Nicolaides. 1983. *Taking the New Protectionism Seriously.* Trade Policy Research Center, Thames Essay no. 34, London.

Hirschman, Albert O. 1981. "The Rise and Decline of Development Economics." In *Essays in Trespassing.* Cambridge, Eng.

Hofheinz, Roy, Jr., and Kent E. Calder. 1982. *The Eastasia Edge.* New York.

Hollerman, Leon, ed. 1980. *Japan and the United States: Economic and Political Adversaries.* Boulder, Colo.

Hong, Wontack. 1984a. "Expansion of Manufactured Exports by Advanced Developing Countries and Its Impact on U.S. and Japan." Mimeo, Seoul University.

———. 1984b. "Growth and Trade with Double Distortions in Developing Economy." Mimeo, Seoul University.

Hong, Wontack, and Lawrence B. Krause, eds. 1981. *Trade and Growth of the Advanced Developing Countries in the Pacific Basin.* Korea Development Institute, Seoul.

Hong Kong. 1984. *A Draft Agreement Between the Government of the United Kingdom of Great Britain and Northern Ireland and the Government of the People's Republic of China on the Future of Hong Kong.* White Paper of Her Majesty's Government, London.

Huan, Hsiang. 1983. "Where Communist China Stands," *Inside China Mainland* (Inst. of Current China Studies, Taipei), Apr.

Hubbard, G. E. 1935. *Eastern Industrialization and Its Effects on the West.* 2d ed. Oxford.

Hufbauer, Gary, ed. 1982. *U.S. International Economic Policy 1981: A Draft Report.* International Law Institute, Washington, D.C.

Hufbauer, Gary C., and Howard Rosen. 1983. "Managing Comparative Disadvantage." Mimeo, Inst. of International Economics, Washington, D.C.

Hughes, H., and J. Waelbroeck. 1981. "Trade and Protection in the 1970's: Can the Growth of Developing-Country Export Continue in the 1980's?" *World Economy,* June, pp. 127-47.

IMF (International Monetary Fund). 1963. *Direction of Trade 1958-62.* Washington, D.C.

———. 1975. *Direction of Trade 1970-74.* Washington, D.C.

———. 1983. *Balance of Payments Statistics Yearbook.* Washington, D.C.

———. 1984a. *Annual Report.* Washington, D.C.

———. 1984b. *Direction of Trade.* Washington, D.C.

ICOT (Institute for New Generation Computer Technology). 1982. "Outline of Research and Development Plans for Fifth Generation Computer Systems," Tokyo.

Japan Economic Planning Agency. 1984. *Annual Report on the Economy: Summary.* Tokyo.

Japan External Trade Organization. 1984. *White Paper on Overseas Markets for 1984.* Tokyo.

Japan Patent Agency. 1983. *Annual Report 1982.* Tokyo.

Japan in the Year 2000. 1983. Long-Term Outlook Committee, Economic Council, Economic Planning Agency, Japan Times, Tokyo.

Japan-United States. 1981. *Report of the Japan-United States Economic Relations Group,* prepared for the President of the United States and the Prime Minister of Japan, with a *Supplementary Report* and with an *Appendix to the Report of the Japan-United States Economic Relations Group.* Washington, D.C.

Johnson, Chalmers. 1982. *MITI and the Japanese Miracle.* Stanford, Calif.

Kahn, Herman. 1970. *The Emerging Japanese Superstate: Challenge and Response.* Englewood Cliffs, N.J.

———. 1982. *The Coming Boom.* New York.

Kahn, Herman, and Thomas Pepper. 1979. *The Japanese Challenge.* New York.

Kaplan, Eugene J. 1972. *Japan: The Government-Business Relationship.* U.S. Bureau of International Commerce, Washington, D.C.

Keesing, Donald B. 1979. *Trade Policy for Developing Countries.* World Bank Staff Working Paper no. 353, Washington, D.C.

Kierzkowski, H. 1980. "Displacement of Labor by Imports of Manufactures," *World Development,* Oct., pp. 753-62.

Kikuchi, Makato. 1983. *Japanese Electronics*. Tokyo.

Kim, Jae-ik. 1983. "The Need for Developing Countries to Play Their Role in the GATT," *World Economy*, Sept., pp. 245-52.

Knaack, Ruud. 1981. "Economic Reform in China," *ACES Bulletin* (Association of Comparative Economic Studies), 23 (2): 1-29.

Knight, Peter T. 1983. *Economic Reform in Socialist Countries*. World Bank Staff Working Paper no. 579, Washington, D.C.

Kohn, Hans. 1934. *Orient and Occident*. New York.

Kojima, Kiyoshi. 1971. *Japan and a Pacific Free Trade Area*. Berkeley, Calif.

————. 1978. *Direct Foreign Investment: A Japanese Model of Multinational Business Operations*. London.

————. 1981. "Japan's Economic Relationship with the Pacific Basin," Mimeo, Hitotsubashi University, Tokyo.

Komiya, Ryutaro. 1982. "The U.S.-Japan Trade Conflict: An Economist's View from Japan." In Okimoto 1982, pp. 197-230.

Krause, Lawrence B. 1982. *U.S. Economic Policy Toward the Association of Southeast Asian Nations: Meeting the Japanese Challenge*. Brookings Institution, Washington, D.C.

Krause, Lawrence B., and Sueo Sekiguchi, eds. 1980. *Economic Interaction in the Pacific Basin*. Brookings Institution, Washington, D.C.

Krauss, Melwyn. 1978. *The New Protectionism: The Welfare State and International Trade*. New York.

————. 1983. *Development Without Aid: Growth, Poverty and Government*. New York.

Krueger, Anne O. 1974. "The Political Economy of the Rent-Seeking Society," *American Economic Review*, June, pp. 291-303.

————. 1977. *Growth, Distortions and Patterns of Trade Among Many Countries*. Princeton, N.J.

————. 1978. *Foreign Trade Regimes and Economic Development: Liberalization Attempts and Consequences*. Cambridge, Mass.

————. 1979. *Studies in the Modernization of Korea: The Developmental Role of the Foreign Sector and Aid*. Cambridge, Mass.

————. 1980a. "Regional and Global Approaches to Trade and Development Strategy." In Garnaut 1980, pp. 21-45.

————. 1980b. "Impact of Foreign Trade on Employment in United States Industry." In *Current Issues in Commercial Policy and Diplomacy*, ed. John Black and Brian Hindley. New York.

————. 1981a. "Export-Led Industrial Growth Reconsidered." In Hong and Krause 1981, pp. 3-27.

————. 1981b. "Loans to Assist the Transition to Outward-Looking Policies," *World Economy*, Sept., pp. 271-81.

————. 1983. *Trade and Employment in Developing Countries*, Vol. 3: *Synthesis and Conclusions*. Chicago.

————. In Press. "Comparative Advantage and Development Policy Twenty Years Later." In *Festschrift in Honor of Hollis B. Chenery*.

Krugman, Paul R. 1984. "The U.S. Response to Foreign Industrial Targeting," *Brookings Papers on Economic Activity*, no. 1, pp. 77-121.

Kuo, Shirley W. Y. 1983. *The Taiwan Economy in Transition.* Boulder, Colo.

Kuo, Shirley W. Y., G. Ranis, and J. C. H. Fei. 1981. *The Taiwan Success Story.* Boulder, Colo.

Kuznets, Simon. 1955. "Economic Growth and Income Inequality," *American Economic Review* 45: 1-28.

———. 1979. "Growth and Structural Shifts." In Galenson 1979, pp. 15-131.

Lach, Donald F. 1965. *Asia in the Making of Europe.* 2 vols. Chicago.

Lal, Deepak. 1982. *Resurrection of the Pauper-Labour Argument.* Trade Policy Research Centre, Thames Essay no. 28, London.

———. 1983. *The Poverty of "Development Economics."* Inst. of Economics Affairs, London.

Landes, David S. 1977. "The 'Great Drain' and Industrialization: Commodity Flows from Periphery to Center in Historical Perspective." Paper read to the World Congress of the International Economic Association, Tokyo.

Lee, Sang M., and Gary Schwendiman, eds. 1982. *Management by Japanese Systems.* New York.

Lee, T. H., and Kuo-shu Liang. 1982. "Taiwan." In Balassa, et al. 1982, pp. 310-50.

Lewis, W. A. 1978. *Growth and Fluctuations, 1870-1913.* London.

———. 1984. "The State of Development Theory," *American Economic Review*, Mar., pp. 1-10.

Li, Dun J. 1965. *The Ageless Chinese.* New York.

Lim, Teck Ghee. 1974. "Southeast Asian Perceptions of Japan and the Japanese." In *Japan as an Economic Power and Its Implications for Southeast Asia*, ed. K. S. Sandhu and Eileen P. T. Tang, pp. 88-96. Singapore.

Lin, Tzong Biau, and Yin Ping Ho. 1981. "Export-Oriented Growth and Industrial Diversification in Hong Kong." In Hong and Krause 1981, pp. 69-123.

Lindbeck, Assar. 1981. "Industrial Policy as an Issue: The Economic Environment," *World Economy*, Dec., pp. 391-405.

Linder, Staffan Burenstam. 1983. *Den Hjaertloesa Vaelfaerdsstaten.* Stockholm.

Lipset, Seymour Martin. 1984. "Report on a Trip to China, May-June, 1984." Mimeo, Hoover Institution, Stanford, Calif.

Little, I. M. D. 1979. *The Experiences and Causes of Rapid-Intensive Development in Kenya, Taiwan, Turkey and Singapore: And the Possibilities of Emulation.* International Labor Organization Working Paper WPII-1, Bangkok.

———. 1982. *Economic Development.* New York.

Little, I. M. D., Tibor Scitovsky, and K. Scott. 1970. *Industry and Trade in Some Developing Countries.* Oxford.

Lynn, Leonard H. 1983. "Technology Transfers to Japan: What We Know, What We Need to Know, and What We Know That May Not Be So." Paper prepared for Conference on International Technology Transfer, June 2-3, New York. Mimeo.

Mackintosh, Malcolm. 1983. "Soviet Attitudes Towards East Asia." In Segal 1983, pp. 6-15.

Magaziner, Ira, and Robert Reich. 1982. *Minding America's Business.* New York.

Mason, Edward S., et al. 1980. *The Economic and Social Modernization of the Republic of Korea.* Cambridge, Mass.

McKinnon, Ronald I. 1973. *Money and Capital in Economic Development.* Brookings Institution, Washington, D.C.

Meier, Gerald. 1984. *Emerging from Poverty.* Oxford.

Miller, William F. 1983a. "Science and World Economic Progress." Mimeo, SRI International, Menlo Park, Calif.

——. 1983b. "Science and Technology–Restructuring the U.S. Economy." Mimeo, SRI International, Menlo Park, Calif.

MITI. 1980. "The Vision of MITI Policies in the 1980's: Trade and Industrial Policy for the 1980's." Mimeo, MITI, Tokyo.

Morishima, Michio. 1982. *Why Has Japan "Succeeded"? Western Technology and Japanese Ethos.* New York.

Morrison, C., and S. Sato. 1984. "Japan and Regionalism." Mimeo.

Myers, Ramon H. 1983. "The Contest Between the Two Chinese States," *Asian Survey,* Apr., pp. 536-51.

——. 1984. "The Pacific Basin." In *Strategies for Peace: The United States Foreign Policy in the Mid-1980's,* ed. Dennis Bork. Stanford, Calif.

Myrdal, Gunnar. 1980. "Noedhjaelp i staellet foer utvecklingsbistaand" [Emergency relief instead of development aid], *Ekonomisk Debatt,* no. 8: 565-69.

Nanto, Richard K. 1982. "Sino-Japanese Economic Relations." In *China Under the Four Modernizations: Selected Papers Submitted to the Joint Economic Committee, Congress of the United States,* pt. 2, 109-26. Washington, D.C.

National Science Board. 1983. *Science Indicators 1982.* Washington, D.C.

Needham, J., and Wang Ling. 1954-70. *Science and Civilization in China.* 7 vols. in 12 parts. Cambridge, Eng.

Nelson, Douglas R. 1981. *The Political Structure of the New Protectionism.* World Bank Staff Working Paper no. 471, Washington, D.C.

Nelson, Richard R. 1982. "Government Stimulus of Technological Progress: Lessons from American History." In *Government and Technical Progress,* ed. Richard R. Nelson, 451-82. New York.

Nishimizu, Mieko. 1980. "Technological Superiority: A Milestone in the Postwar Japanese Growth." In Hollerman 1980, pp. 13-37.

Norbury, Paul, and Geoffrey Brownas, eds. 1980. *Business in Japan: A Guide to Japanese Business Practice and Procedure.* Boulder, Colo.

Oborne, Michael West, and Nicolas Fourt. 1983. *Pacific Basin Economic Cooperation.* OECD, Paris.

OECD (Organization for Economic Cooperation and Development). 1979a. *Trends in Industrial R&D in Selected Member Countries, 1967-1975.* Paris.

――――. 1979b. *The Impact of the Newly-Industrializing Countries on Production and Trade in Manufactures.* Paris.

――――. 1980. *Technical Change and Economic Policy.* Paris.

――――. 1981. *The Impact of the Newly Industrializing Countries: Updating of Selected Tables from the 1979 Report.* Paris.

――――. 1982a. *Positive Adjustment Policies: Final Report, Introduction, Summary and Conclusions.* Paris.

――――. 1982b. *Economic Outlook, 1982.* Paris.

――――. 1983. *World Economic Interdependence and the Evolving North-South Relationship.* Paris.

――――. 1984a. *Economic Outlook.* Paris.

――――. 1984b. *National Accounts.* Paris.

――――. Development Assistance Committee. 1980. *Development Cooperation.* Paris.

――――. 1981. *Development Co-operation.* Paris.

――――. 1982. *Development Co-operation.* Paris.

Ohira Report, *see* Pacific Basin Cooperation Study Group.

Okimoto, Daniel I., ed. 1982. *Japan's Economy, Coping with Change in the International Environment.* Boulder, Colo.

――――. 1983. *Pioneer and Pursuer: The Role of the State in the Evolution of the Japanese and American Semiconductor Industries.* Northeast Asia-United States Forum of International Policy, Stanford University.

――――. 1984. "Instruments of Japanese Industrial Policy for High Technology: The Information Industry." Paper prepared for the Conference on Japanese Industrial Policy in Comparative Perspective, Mar. 17-19, New York. Mimeo.

Okimoto, Daniel I., and Gary R. Saxonhouse. 1983. "From Smokestack to Hi Tech: Japanese Technology in Transition." Mimeo, Northeast Asia-United States Forum on International Policy, Stanford University.

Olechowski, Andrzej, and Gary Sampson. 1980. "Current Trade Restrictions in the EEC, the United States and Japan," *Journal of World Trade Law,* May-June, pp. 220-31.

Olson, Mancur. 1982. *The Rise and Decline of Nations.* New Haven, Ct.

Ouchi, William. 1981. *Theory Z: How American Business Can Meet the Japanese Challenge.* Reading, Mass.

Ozawa, Terutomo. 1979. *Multinationalism, Japanese Style: The Political Economy of Outward Dependency.* Princeton, N.J.

――――. 1983. "Macroeconomic Factors Affecting Technology Inflows to and Outflows from Japan: The Postwar Experience." Paper presented to the Conference on International Technology Transfer, June 2-3, New York. Mimeo.

Pacific Basin Cooperation Study Group. 1980. *Report on the Pacific Basin Cooperation Concept* (the "Ohira Report"). Tokyo.

Panikkar, K. M. 1953. *Asia and Western Dominance*. London.

Park, Pil-Soo. 1983. "Summary Note, Experiences of Industrial Restructuring in the Republic of Korea." U.N. Industrial Development Organization seminar in Thailand. Mimeo.

Pascale, R. and A. G. Athos. 1981. *The Art of Japanese Management*. New York.

Patrick, Hugh. 1981. "U.S.-Chinese Economic Relations in the Asian Pacific Context," *World Economy*, June, pp. 149-74.

———. 1982. "The Economic Dimensions of the U.S.-Japan Alliance: An Overview." In Okimoto 1982, pp. 149-98.

Patrick, Hugh, and Peter Drysdale. 1983. "A Proposal on the Pacific Trade and Development Conference (PACTAD) Series and the Establishment of a PACTAD Secretariat." Mimeo.

Patrick, Hugh, and Henry Rosovsky, eds. 1976. *Asia's New Giant—How the Japanese Economy Works*. Brookings Institution, Washington, D.C.

Patterson, Gardner. 1966. *Discrimination in International Trade: The Policy Issues 1945-1965*. Princeton, N.J.

Paukert, F. 1973. "Income Distribution at Different Levels of Development: A Survey of Evidence." *International Labour Review* 108(2-3): 97-125.

Rabushka, Alvin. 1979. *Hong Kong, A Study in Economic Freedom*. Chicago.

———. 1984. "From Adam Smith to the Wealth of America." Mimeo, Hoover Institution, Stanford, Calif.

Rao, V. V. Bhanoji, and M. K. Ramakrishnan. 1976. "Economic Growth, Structural Change and Income Inequality, Singapore, 1966-1975," *The Malayan Economic Review*, Oct., pp. 92-122.

Rawski, Thomas G. 1982. "The Simple Arithmetic of Chinese Income Distribution," *Keizai Kenkyu* (The Economic Review) (Hitotsubashi University), Jan., pp. 12-26.

Republic of China. 1984. *Statistical Yearbook*. Taipei.

Reynolds, Bruce L. 1982. "Reform in Chinese Industrial Management: An Empirical Report." In *China Under the Four Modernizations, Selected Papers Submitted to the Joint Economic Committee, Congress of the United States*, Aug. 13, pp. 119-37. Washington, D.C.

Riedel, James. 1983. *Trade as an Engine of Growth in Developing Countries: A Reappraisal*. World Bank Staff Working Paper no. 555, Washington, D.C.

Rosenberg, Nathan. 1982. *Inside the Black Box: Technology and Economics*. Cambridge, Eng.

Rosenberg, Nathan, and L. E. Birdzell, Jr. 1985. *How the West Grew Rich: The Escape from Poverty*. New York.

Rostow, Walt W. E. 1985. "Is There Need for Economic Leadership: Japanese or U.S.?" *American Economic Review*, May.

Saxonhouse, Gary R. 1982a. "Cyclical and Macrostructural Issues in U.S.-Japan Economic Relations." In Okimoto 1982, pp. 123-48.

———. 1982b. "Evolving Comparative Advantage and Japan's Imports of Manufactures." In Yamamura 1982, pp. 239-70.

———. 1983a. "What Is All This About 'Industrial Targeting' in Japan?" *World Economy*, Sept., pp. 253-73.

———. 1983b. "The Micro- and Macroeconomics of Foreign Sales to Japan." In Cline 1983, pp. 259-304.

Scalapino, Robert A. 1982. "The Political Influence of the USSR in Asia." In Zagoria 1982, pp. 57-92.

Schultz, Theodore W. 1981. "Economic Distortions by the International Donor Community," *Academia Economic Papers* (Taipei), Mar., pp. 57-67.

Schultze, Charles L. 1983. "Industrial Policy: A Dissent," *The Brookings Review*, Fall, pp. 3-12.

Scitovsky, Tibor. 1982. "Economic Development in Taiwan and South Korea: 1965-1980. A Comparison." Mimeo, Stanford University.

Segal, Gerald, ed. 1983. *The Soviet Union in East Asia*. Boulder, Colo.

Sekiguchi, Sueo. 1979. *Japan's Direct Foreign Investment*. Japan Economic Research Center, Tokyo.

———. 1982. "Japan's Direct Investment in Europe." In Tsoukalis and White 1982, pp. 166-83.

Shephard, Geoffrey. 1981. "The Japanese Challenge to Western Europe's New Crisis Industries," *World Economy*, Dec., pp. 375-90.

Siriboon, Nawadhinsukh. 1983. *Industrial Restructuring in the Automotive Industry*. Industrial Management Co., Bangkok.

Solinger, Dorothy J. 1981. "Economic Reform via Reformulation in China: Where Do Rightist Ideas Come From?" *Asian Survey*, 21(9): 947-60.

Spraos, J. 1980. "The Statistical Debate on the Net Barter Terms of Trade Between Primary Commodities and Manufactures," *Economic Journal*, Mar., pp. 107-28.

Squire, L. 1981. *Employment Policy in Developing Countries—A Survey of Issues and Evidence*. Oxford.

Stern, Fritz. 1977. "The Giant from Afar—Visions of Europe from Algiers to Tokyo," *Foreign Affairs*, Oct., pp. 111-35.

Streeten, Paul. 1982. "A Cool Look at 'Outward-looking' Strategies for Development," *World Economy*, Sept., pp. 159-69.

Tan, Augustine H. H., and Ow Chin Hock. 1982. "Singapore." In Balassa, et al. 1982, pp. 280-309.

Tasca, Diane, ed. 1980. *U.S.-Japanese Economic Relations: Cooperation, Competition, and Confrontation*. New York.

Thompson, James C., Peter W. Stanley and John Curtis Perry. 1981. *Sentimental Imperialists: The American Experience in East Asia*. New York.

Thompson, Richard Austin. 1978. *The Yellow Peril, 1890-1924*. New York.

Trade Policy Research Centre. 1981. *Global Strategy for Growth, A Report on North-South Issues*. TPRC, Special Report no. 1, London.

———. 1983. *In the Kingdom of the Blind*. A Report on Protectionism and the Asian-Pacific Region. TPRC, Special Report no. 3, London.

Trezise, Philip H. 1983. "Industrial Policy Is Not the Major Reason for Japan's Success," *The Brookings Review*, Spring, pp. 13-18.

Tsoukalis, Loukas, and Maureen White, eds. 1982. *Japan and Western Europe: Conflict and Cooperation*. London.

Turner, Louis, Neil McMullen, et al. 1982. *The Newly Industrializing Countries: Trade and Adjustment*. London.

Tyler, William C. 1981. "Growth and Export Expansion in Developing Countries: Some Empirical Evidence," *Journal of Development Economics*, Aug., pp. 121-30.

U.N. (United Nations). 1966. *Yearbook of International Trade Statistics 1964*. New York.

———. 1976. *Yearbook of International Trade Statistics 1974*. New York.

———. 1983. *Yearbook of National Account Statistics 1981*. New York.

———. 1984. *Yearbook of International Trade Statistics 1982*. New York.

U.N. ESCAP (Economic and Social Commission for Asia and the Pacific). 1984. *Yearbook for Asia and the Pacific 1982*. Bangkok.

UNCTAD (U.N. Conference on Trade and Development). 1983a. *Protectionism, Trade Relations and Structural Adjustment*. Report by the UNCTAD Secretariat for UNCTAD VI. TD/274, Jan. 7.

———. 1983b. *Handbook of International Trade and Development Statistics*. New York.

U.S. Bureau of the Census. 1984. *Statistical Abstract of the United States, 1984*. Washington, D.C.

U.S. Council of Economic Advisers. 1984. *Economic Report of the President Together with the Annual Report of the Council of Economic Advisers*. Washington, D.C.

U.S. International Trade Commission. 1983. *Foreign Industrial Targeting and Its Effects on U.S. Industries. Phase I: Japan*. Washington, D.C.

———. 1984. *Foreign Industrial Targeting and Its Effects on U.S. Industries. Phase II: The European Community and Member States*. Washington, D.C.

Vasey, Lloyd R., and George J. Viksnins, eds. 1976. *The Economic and Political Growth Pattern of Asia-Pacific*. Honolulu.

Vermeer, E. B. 1982. "Income Differentials in Rural China," *The China Quarterly*, Mar., pp. 1-33. See also Comments and Reply, by Keith Griffin and E. B. Vermeer respectively, in *The China Quarterly*, Dec. 1982, pp. 706-13.

Verreydt, E., and J. Waelbroeck. 1980. *European Community Protection Against Manufactured Imports from Developing Countries: A Case Study in the Political Economy of Protection*. World Bank Staff Working Paper no. 432, Washington, D.C.

Vogel, Ezra. 1979. *Japan as Number One: Lessons for America*. Cambridge, Mass.

Waelbroeck, Jean. 1983. "The 'SPELC'–A Tale of Post-war Western Europe," *The World Economy* 6(4): 409-20.

Wang, Georg C., ed. 1982. *Economic Reform in PRC*. Boulder, Colo.

Weber, Max. 1951. *The Religion of China*. Glencoe, Ill.

Weitzman, Martin L. 1984. *The Share Economy*. Cambridge, Mass.

Weston, Ann, Vincent Cable, and Adrian Hewitt. 1980. *The EEC's Generalized System of Preferences–Evaluation and Recommendations for Change*. Overseas Development Inst., London.

Westphal, Larry, and Kwang Suk Kim. 1977. *Industrial Policy and Development in Korea*. World Bank Staff Working Paper no. 263, Washington, D.C.

———. 1982. "Korea." In Balassa et al. 1982, pp. 212-79.

White, Merry I. 1984. "Japanese Education: How Do They Do It?," *The Public Interest*, Summer, pp. 87-110.

Wilkinson, Endymion. 1981. *Misunderstanding, Europe Versus Japan*. Tokyo.

———. 1983. *What Are the Implications of the Development in the Pacific Basin for the Old Industrial Nations of Western Europe*. Scandinavian Pacific Inst., Stockholm.

Wolf, Martin. 1979. *Adjustment Policies and Problems in Developed Countries*. World Bank Staff Working Paper no. 349, Washington, D.C.

World Bank. 1982. *Trade and Employment Policies for Industrial Development*. Economics and Research Staff, ERS/MC83-05, World Bank, Washington, D.C.

———. 1983a. *World Development Report 1983*. Oxford.

———. 1983b. "Trade Policy Issues." Mimeo, Economics and Research Staff, June 21, Washington, D.C.

———. 1983c. *World Tables*, Vol. 1: *Economic Data*. 3d ed. Baltimore.

———. 1984. *World Development Report 1984*. Oxford.

Wu, Yuan-li. 1983. "Chinese Entrepreneurs in Southeast Asia," *American Economic Review*, May, pp. 112-17.

Wu, Yuan-li, and Chun-hsi Wu. 1980. *Economic Development in Southeast Asia: The Chinese Dimension*. Stanford, Calif.

Yamamura, Kozo. 1982. *Policies and Trade Issues of the Japanese Economy, American and Japanese Perspectives*. Seattle.

Yasuba, Yasukichi. 1980. "The Impact of ASEAN on the Asia-Pacific Region." In Garnaut 1980, pp. 73-96.

Yoffie, David B. 1983. *Power and Protectionism, Strategies of the Newly Industrializing Countries*. New York.

Yoffie, David B., and Robert Keohane. 1981. "Responding to the 'New Protectionism': Strategies for the ADCs." In Hong and Krause 1981, pp. 560-89.

Zagoria, Donald S., ed. 1982. *Soviet Policy in East Asia*. New Haven, Ct.

Zhou Bin. 1982. "Japanese Studies in China," *The Japan Foundation Newsletter* 10 (4): 1-7.

Index

Library of Congress Cataloging-in-Publication Data

Linder, Staffan Burenstam, 1931-
    The Pacific century.

    Bibliography: p.
    Includes index.
    1. Pacific Area—Economic conditions.   2. Pacific
Area—Politics and government.   I. Title.
HC681.L56   1986   330.9182'3   85-22053
ISBN 0-8047-1294-8 (alk. paper)
ISBN 0-8047-1305-7 (pbk.: alk. paper)